NIAGARA'S GOLD

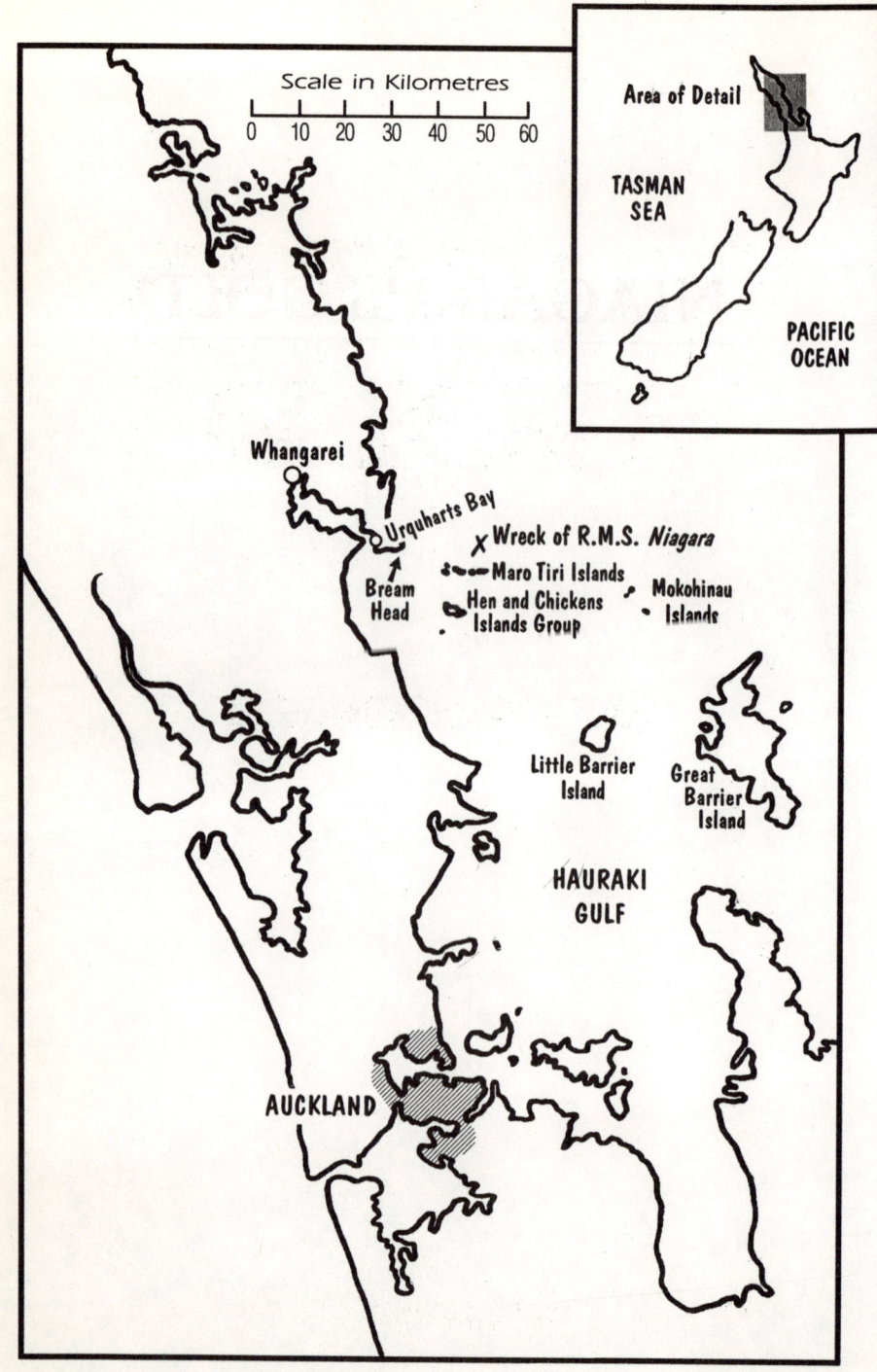

NIAGARA'S GOLD

JEFF MAYNARD

Kangaroo Press

For Zoe
Who throughout the difficult years of its research and writing never once questioned that this was a story worth salvaging.

Jeff Maynard

Jeff Maynard is a freelance writer who has previously published books of poetry and prose, written for televison, edited magazines and had articles published around the world. While researching and writing *Niagara's Gold* he also wrote and co-produced a television documentary of the same name.

By the same author:

Memorials
The Letterbox War of Kamarooka Street

Cover art by John Gibson
Design by Darian Causby

© Jeff Maynard 1996

Reprinted 1996
First published in 1996 by Kangaroo Press Pty Ltd
3 Whitehall Road Kenthurst NSW 2156 Australia
P.O. Box 6125 Dural Delivery Centre NSW 2158
Printed by Australian Print Group, Maryborough, 3465

ISBN 0 86417 7666

Contents

Foreword 6

1. She's a Grand Old Lady and She's Dying Gracefully 7
2. A Regular Millionaire's Yacht 23
3. When a Beggar He Prepares to Plunge 39
4. A Finer Lot of Chaps I Have Never Met 55
5. The Job Would Not Be Very Complicated 68
6. What's That in Those Cases? 78
7. Winter Is On Us in Earnest 88
8. A Piece of Precision Machinery 106
9. When a Prince He Rises with his Pearl 121
10. Any Honour You Like to Name 133

Afterword 151
Acknowledgments 154
References 155
Index 157

Foreword

In June 1940, shortly before the Battle of Britain, the Bank of England attempted to ship eight tons of gold to America to buy arms for the war against Germany.

On 18 June, the ship carrying the gold, the RMS *Niagara*, hit a German mine and sank in deep water off the coast of New Zealand.

In the months that followed one man would invent a way of working up to 600 feet underwater, assemble a crew—Canadians, Australians, Englishmen, New Zealanders—aged between 16 and 75, refloat a rusting coastal steamer, then sail the lot into the middle of a minefield to begin searching for the *Niagara*.

The remarkable story that followed has never been told . . .

Author's Note

Because all of the records, including the *Claymore*'s logbook, used fathoms and feet instead of metres, inches instead of centimetres, pounds, shillings and pence instead of dollars and cents, tons instead of tonnes and so on, I have used imperial measures, weights and British/Australian currency values throughout the book for authenticity. Where I've considered it might be useful for the reader I have included the metric or decimal equivalent in the text. A fathom, for those not familiar with the term, is six feet or 1.8288 metres.

ONE

The Present – 19 June 1940

She's a Grand Old Lady and She's Dying Gracefully

Danny Scott died on 31 January 1991. It wasn't until six months later that I realised the significance of this date or what a remarkable coincidence it was. When he died, Danny Scott was 93 years old. He had spent his last twelve years in an old persons' home in the Melbourne suburb of Footscray. During that time he had given away most of his personal possessions so all he had left was a small box containing some old letters and yellowing newspaper clippings.

His death would have gone unnoticed had not a friend contacted a local newspaper and told Danny's story. On 12 February 1991 the *Western Independent* ran an article featuring a photograph of Danny Scott. Above it the headline read 'Danny Scott was the last survivor of the RMS *Niagara* gold expedition.'

Being a local resident I saw the article. As a freelance writer in the middle of a recession I saw an opportunity to sell a story. It was the fiftieth anniversary of the 'expedition' and the passing of the last survivor was surely newsworthy. I had a 1942 book on the subject and so wrote an article. Then I rang the *Sydney Morning Herald*. I thought they might be interested because they had sent a journalist to cover the story in 1941. I was told that the *Sydney Morning Herald* was part of the Fairfax Group, which was in receivership, and as a consequence was not accepting articles from freelance writers. I tried other papers and magazines. The best offer I could get was $400 from The *Australasian Post*.

The *Australasian Post* is a weekly pictorial magazine read by men waiting for a haircut or taxi drivers waiting for a fare. It derives most of its editorial thrust from naked breasts and most of its advertising revenue from people selling army memorabilia or condoms. I had never written for it before and didn't imagine I'd look back on it as a career highlight.

I had called the story '*Claymore's* Heroes' but they did not consider this sensational enough and renamed it 'Bullion Bonanza'. In the same issue were stories on 'Nude Olympics' in Western Australia and a man who was a werewolf.

I hoped no one would see my by-line, filed my copy, cashed my cheque and thought the matter finished. Two weeks later I got a letter in the mail. It had been sent to the editor of the *Post* who had forwarded it on to me. It read:

Australasian Post,
Dear Editor,

I was most interested to read an article in the *Post* titled 'Bullion Bonanza', by Jeff Maynard. I refer especially to the last paragraph and the death of Bosun Danny Scott, 'the last surviving member of this remarkable team'.

That is not correct. I am still around and active on my farm at the above address. I commenced work with Captain Williams in the Maryborough District about 1933, goldmining. I was in Western Australia when the 'Niagara' was sunk and at Captain Williams' invitation returned to Melbourne and joined the salvage team. I was one of the original team to go to New Zealand and saw the job through from start to finish. If you look at the picture, page 8 bottom left, I am the man in the centre behind the stack of gold.

As far as I know the only other member of the team, apart from myself, who may be alive is Bill Johnstone, the chap in the naval uniform in the second picture. I lost touch with Bill just after the War. When Captain Williams died just over 2 years ago I had known and kept in touch with him for 56 years.

Sorry to cause a problem but I can't let this go by without correction.
Yours faithfully,
Arthur J. Bryant

For the next four years I followed the story of the recovery of the gold from the RMS *Niagara*. It is a story of incredible fortune—

both good and bad—of irony and betrayal, of courage and ingenuity.

It is also the story of two men—Captain John Protheroe Williams and diver John Edward Johnstone—who began, if not as friends, then at least as working partners. But who, despite living in the same city for over 30 years until Johnstone's death, were never to speak to one another again.

But all this I was to learn later. For the story of the greatest gold salvage in history really began in the dark month of June 1940.

* * *

The rise of Adolf Hitler and the series of events that led to World War II have been recorded many times. Few aspects of the war have not been covered by 'official' histories, personal memoirs, television documentaries, glossy coffee-table picture books or Hollywood-style motion pictures. Therefore it's necessary here to write no more than a brief recap of the events that led to the crisis of May and June 1940.

In 1933 Hitler had been appointed Chancellor of Germany. A year later he was made both Chancellor and President—two titles that gave him a dictatorship over a country which had been beaten in World War I, stripped of much of its territory, and which languished in economic depression.

Hitler immediately began increasing the military strength of Germany. In 1935 he reintroduced conscription. In 1936 Italy became an ally of Germany after the formation of the Rome-Berlin Axis. In the same year the Anti-Comitern (anti-communist) Pact was signed with Japan. Germany, Italy and Japan marched steadily towards war with the rest of the world. By 1938 Hitler was ready to start taking back what he felt was stolen from Germany at the end of World War I. Germany annexed Austria. Then it annexed the Sudetan district of Czechoslovakia. In March 1939 Hitler proclaimed Bohemia and Moravia German protectorates. Lithuania ceded Memel to Germany. On 1 September Germany invaded Poland. On 3 September, Great Britain declared war on Germany.

But despite war being declared, nothing happened. Hitler, temporarily, stopped advancing. Across the border between France and Germany opposing armies looked at each other, but no one fired their guns. This 'Phoney War' lasted eight months.

Then, at 5.30 a.m. on 10 May 1940, Europe erupted into bloody conflict. At that time Germany invaded Holland, Belgium and Luxembourg. The same day Winston Churchill became Prime Minister of England. In the following weeks city after city fell as the German Army swarmed over Europe. Their tanks rolled into France. The British Army, which had been in Europe during the Phoney War was surrounded and driven to the sea at Dunkirk. The German Army marched into Paris and France capitulated. Britain evacuated its troops from the beaches of Dunkirk. In a little over four weeks Hitler had conquered Western Europe. Only the tiny British Islands, separated from the mainland by the narrow English Channel, had not surrendered.

Britain was hopelessly unprepared for war, but it had two strengths. One, it was an island nation. Hitler could drive his tanks across Europe but he couldn't drive them across water. The other strength was the British dominions. Countries of the Commonwealth. Canada, India, Australia, South Africa, New Zealand and others, spread in so many places around the globe that in 1940 it was possible to circumnavigate the world sailing on nothing but British ships or walking on nothing but British soil. The dominions could supply Britain with food and clothing, tanks and planes, armies and guns. And they could also supply a lifeline to the manufacturing might of the United States of America. But only if the sea routes to them could be kept open to shipping.

Of all these dominions, none is further from Britain than New Zealand. It is almost at the diametrically opposite point on the globe. And it was here on 13 and 14 June 1940, while the German Army was marching into Paris, the seeds of World War II were being sown in the Southern Hemisphere.

*   *   *

The idea of the raider, or auxiliary cruiser, is a simple one. It is to disguise a ship as a peaceful merchant or passenger ship, but to have it fitted with means of destroying other ships—either by laying mines or by firing guns or torpedoes at them. The raider can sail unchallenged into waters denied the naval vessel, then maintaining its deception get close to an enemy ship. Once close enough to open fire the raider would 'with due regard to the laws and usages of war' reveal itself to be a fighting ship and then open fire on the enemy. Using these same powers of deception the raider could also sail close to enemy ports and, if unchallenged, lay a minefield.

Strictly speaking, it is possible to find examples of this type of naval warfare throughout history. But it became strategically important during World War I. As in World War II, Britain was reliant on supplies from its Empire to sustain its war effort. Germany used raiders to try and cut off those supplies, particularly from Australia and New Zealand. The German U-boat (submarine) was successful in menacing merchant shipping in the North Atlantic, but the U-boat did not have the range to operate in the far-away South Pacific. Raiders such as the *Emden*, *Wolf*, *Cormoran*, *Friedrich*, *Prinz Eitel* and *Seeadler* inflicted great losses in the seas around Australia and New Zealand.

In World War II, Germany realised the advantages of raiders and placed more emphasis on their manning and fitting. Likewise, the Allies knew the potential threat of the raiders and were more observant in their inspection of supposedly neutral ships.

In World War II, if the commander of a raider was going to escape detection, he had to ensure his disguise was near perfect. For this reason carpenters and painters were included in the crew. Overnight they could build a false funnel to make their single-funnel steamer appear a two-funnel ship. And the painters would have the funnels painted in the colours of the shipping line to which they were pretending to belong. Even the crew would be disguised. The *Atlantis*, for example, was provided with Japanese women's clothing and prams, so that when it was posing as a Japanese liner, the crew could dress as women and stroll along the deck.

And such detail, it became obvious, was necessary. The *Pinguin* was sunk by HMS *Cornwall* on 8 May 1941. Posing as a British cargo vessel, the *Cornwall* had her scout plane fly over the *Pinguin* to examine her and the pilot reported that everything looked in order—except that the crew were all white. British cargo vessels invariably had black crew members. The *Pinguin* was exposed.

The use of raiders became as controversial as their methods were cunning. To many Britons, 'it just wasn't cricket'. The idea of being disguised as a neutral merchant or passenger ship, sailing close to another ship, then suddenly hoisting the flag of the German Navy, revealing guns and sinking that ship, which was often a passenger ship with women and children on board, wasn't what warfare was all about. But in World War II Germany would made good use of raiders. The first was the *Orion*.

Formerly the *Kurmark* of the Hamburg-America Line, the *Orion* was 7 800 tons and had a top speed of 12 knots. To the German Navy she was referred to simply as 'Ship 36'. To the Allies, when they came to recognise her as the first enemy ship to reach the South Pacific in the war, she was known as Raider 'A'.

The *Orion* was well equipped for her voyage. She carried 228 mines which she hoped to lay in Auckland Harbour, New Zealand. She had six 5.9 inch guns. Four of these were on the forward deck hidden behind collapsible crating. The other two were on the rear deck, one disguised as a dummy deckhouse, the other left exposed as it was common for merchant ships to carry at least one stern gun in times of war. Two .79 inch guns were carried at the bow and covered with canvas. Two more were carried in the bridge. Two at the rear of the superstructure were disguised as ventilators. And two at the stern were hidden under the poop deck. The *Orion* was also able to fire torpedoes. 'Doors' on the starboard side could swing open to reveal three torpedo tubes. For reconnaissance the *Orion* carried a seaplane hidden in its hold. This could be brought on deck, assembled and lowered over the side so the pilot could take off on a calm sea. To alter the appearance of the ship, large steel plates were carried which could be stood against the funnel to make it look as if it was angled instead of upright. The height of the derricks could be altered or they could be removed completely.

The *Orion* was also well manned. Unlike the raiders of the World War I, whose crews consisted of large numbers of the less experienced navy reservists, the *Orion* had 14 'active' and 6 'reserve' officers, while its 356 petty officers and men were drawn from the regular German Navy. Its commanding officer was 39-year-old Kurt Weyher.

SHE'S A GRAND OLD LADY AND SHE'S DYING GRACEFULLY

On 6 April 1940, Weyher sailed from Suder Piep on the west coast Schleswig-Holstein. The *Orion* was disguised as a two-funnelled navy auxiliary vessel. Seaman Paul Schimdt sat inside the false rear funnel burning oily rags to produce smoke. Thus the *Orion* successfully stole through the British blockade using the first of over twenty false identities it would assume. After only eighteen days at sea the *Orion* found its first victim. On 24 April Weyher received orders to cause a diversion by holding up ships in the North Atlantic. He engaged and sank the British ship *Haxby*. The *Haxby* sent in error the signal RRRR (I am under attack by a warship) rather than QQQQ (I am under attack by a raider). This small error in making the distinction between a warship and a raider meant the *Orion* could continue without British naval authorities realising a raider was heading for the South Pacific. It was a stroke of good fortune for the *Orion* and its audacious captain, but only the first of many.

On 21 May the raider rounded Cape Horn. Weyher's subsequent report explained what happened:

With the rounding of Cape Horn the armed merchant cruiser entered the Pacific. On account of the E-W current a great circle bearing was not steered to New Zealand but first of all to 40 degrees south and from there westwards, in the hope of reaching Auckland by the night of 6/7 June when the moon would be full. This hope was not fulfilled however, because, due to the bad weather, speed had frequently to be reduced and course repeatedly altered. Thus it was only on the 13th June that the ship reached the area where the mines were to be laid.

At 1200 hours on the 13th June the auxiliary cruiser was ... about 150 German nautical miles east of the entrance to Hauraki Gulf. Numerous radio signals and orders were heard from Auckland radio broadcasting to patrol boats at sea. A message from Wellington radio indicated that the Royal New Zealand Air Force was training in the Wellington area.

The weather was particularly unfavourable for the undertaking; cloudless sky, visibility about 12 German nautical miles. A bright moonlight night could be depended upon; moon at first quarter, wind from SW strength 1.

With these weather conditions and the possibility that patrol boats would be operating in Hauraki Gulf the mine laying would have to be carried out at its entrance. It was not possible to approach closer than 8 German nautical miles to the Cuvier lighthouse without being sighted by the signal station.

In all 228 mines were laid. The first mine was laid at 1926 hours in front of the northern entrance to Hauraki Gulf. During the operation three outward bound steamers and one inbound vessel were sighted. As it happened, the mine laying track which had been selected lay well away from the steamers and this fact combined with the clouding of the sky at 2300 hours allowed the mine barrage to be laid unnoticed and without incident.

*   *   *

The Union Steam Ship Company commenced in 1875 when James Mills bought a steamer of 174 tons and began trading between the coastal ports of the young colony of New Zealand. He named his steamer *Maori* and began a Union Steam Ship Company tradition of naming all their ships with *Maori* names. One of the few exceptions was to be the *Niagara*.

With a combination of hard work and vision, James Mills built up his company to a point where, by 1900, it operated over twenty vessels. The company's first passenger service was between the New Zealand cities of Wellington and Christchurch and it was to maintain this service for almost 100 years. Later it began carrying passengers across the Tasman Sea to the Australian ports of Sydney and Melbourne.

At the turn of the century the Union Steam Ship Company secured part of the Royal Mail contract to deliver mail between Australia and Canada. It was to begin a period of prosperity and expansion to the shipping company.

But while the Pacific Ocean passenger routes were being opened up, luxury liners were already crossing the Atlantic. Huge floating hotels, they boasted levels of comfort for passengers never available in the fast-disappearing sailing ships.

To provide passengers in the Pacific with a means of travel to rival the great liners of the Atlantic, the Union Steam Ship Company ordered the construction of its largest ship. To be built by John

SHE'S A GRAND OLD LADY AND SHE'S DYING GRACEFULLY

Brown and Co. of Glasgow, Scotland, it would be 522 feet long, 66 feet wide with a draught of 28 feet. It would have a gross tonnage of 13 415 tons. It would have four passenger decks able to accommodate 281 first-class, 223 second-class and 191 third-class passengers. Its hull would be painted grey, the superstructure white, and it would proudly display the red and black funnels of the Union Steam Ship Company.

Conscious of the importance of the Canadian end of their passenger route, the company decided to break with the tradition of giving their ships Maori names. Instead, the most magnificent ship to sail the Pacific Ocean would be called *Ottawa*. When it was discovered this name was not available, *Sicamous* was chosen. This second choice caused concern among the company's management. Australian and New Zealand passengers were notorious for awarding nicknames to ships. Already the company was not pleased that the *Miowera* was known as 'Weary Mary'. There seemed little doubt that the Sicamous would instantly be known as the 'Sick Mouse', which was hardly a fitting name for such a grand liner.

The name *Niagara* was chosen. It was an especially good choice, management thought. Because Niagara Falls was on the border between Canada and the United States of America, the name would pay a compliment to both countries.

The RMS *Niagara* was launched in Scotland on 17 March 1912. A contemporary newspaper called it the '*Titanic* of the Pacific', but after the real *Titanic* sank a few weeks later the title was not used again. The *Niagara* reached Australia and left on its maiden voyage on 5 May 1913.

Twenty-seven years, one month and eight days later, while the *Orion* was sowing the minefield in the Hauraki Gulf, the Royal Mail Steamer *Niagara*, prepared to cross the Pacific yet again.

On board would be Air Vice-Marshall S. J. Goble, travelling to Canada to take up the post of Empire Air Scheme Liaison Officer, and Mrs Goble, Wilfred Wise MLC and Mrs Wise, Dr J. G. Inkster, a prominent Toronto Minister and Mrs Inkster, three Belgian wool buyers returning to their homeland to fight the Germans, Chinese merchants bound for Fiji, nurses and soldiers, businessmen and working men, mothers and children. In all, 146 passengers embarked with a crew of 203 under Captain William Martin.

The *Niagara* followed the common practice of designating its decks alphabetically, A-deck being the uppermost. Below D-deck were the engine rooms, boilers and cargo holds.

The steward's room, where valuable silverware was stored, was on D-deck, between the first-class accommodation (surely the people least likely to steal something) and the forward funnel. Beside the steward's room, located more in the centre of the *Niagara*, was the room where the most valuable things of all were carried—the bullion room. On this journey the bullion room would carry a special cargo.

Gold bars, each weighing 400 troy ounces or 33.333 troy pounds (12.44 kilograms). Each bar about the size of a house brick. Each bar freshly minted at the Rand in South Africa and each bearing a four-digit serial number prefixed by the letters AU, an abbreviation of aurum, the Latin for gold. The bars were stowed two per pine box. 295 pine boxes. 590 bars. Total weight was over eight imperial tons, or almost seven and a half metric tonnes.

At a time when working men earned £2 per week, each bar was worth £4 230. And each bar was the property of the Bank of England ... property which was being sent to the United States of America where it could be kept out of the reach of Adolf Hitler and, if necessary, used to purchase war materials.

Thus the *Niagara* sailed out of Sydney on 13 June 1940. So faithfully had she carried out her duties for the previous 27 years that by this time she had travelled 2 295 000 miles. More than any other passenger ship in the world.

*   *   *

After the last German mine had been laid at the entrance to Auckland Harbour on 14 June Weyher ordered 'full speed ahead' on a bearing of 50 degrees. Five days later the *Orion* was 400 miles away, firing a salvo from her guns at the Norwegian trader *Tropic Sea*. The *Tropic Sea* was carrying 8 100 tons of Australian wheat out of Sydney and as she had suffered no damage Weyher decided to send her to Germany. This plan was abandoned three months later when a British submarine intercepted the *Tropic Sea* and the German crew, now in charge, scuttled her.

Weyher's daring exploits continued. On 16 August he sank the French ship *Notou* (2 489 tons) off New Caledonia. There were no casualties. Four days later, using her torpedoes, the *Orion* sank the New Zealand ship *Turakina* (8 706 tons), thirty-six crew were killed and 21 taken prisoner. After refuelling at the Marshall Islands the *Orion* sank the Norwegian ship *Ringwood* (7 302 tons) with no casualties, taking 36 prisoners. On 18 October 1940 she arrived at Lamutrik in the Caroline Islands to join the raider *Komet*.

For the next two months the *Orion* and the *Komet*, assisted by a smaller supply ship wreaked havoc. They sank the New Zealand ship *Holmwood* (546 tons) on 25 November. Two days later they got their biggest prize, when the 16 712 ton passenger liner *Rangitane,* bound for London, was sunk with a combination of gunfire and torpedoes. Five people were killed and 303 prisoners taken. By intercepting radio traffic the *Orion* and *Komet* then learnt of the arrival of phosphate ships at the island of Nauru. They sailed north and together sank five ships in two days. By this time their holds were bulging with 675 prisoners, including 52 women and three children.

It was decided to put these prisoners ashore. On 19 December 1940, to the astonishment of the lone copra planter who inhabited it, 514 prisoners were put ashore on the island of Emirau in the Bismarck Archipelago. The commander of the *Komet*, Robert Eyssen, then did something that would later incur the wrath of his Nazi superiors in Berlin. He radioed the Australian Navy in Sydney and asked them to come and pick the people up.

At this point the joint operations between the *Orion* and the *Komet* concluded. The *Orion* sailed to the Caroline Islands, where her engines were overhauled. She then sailed south, around Australia and into the Indian Ocean. She spent two fruitless months looking for victims before rounding the Cape of Good Hope and heading north into the Atlantic. In the Atlantic she surprised and sank the British ship *Chaucer* (5 792 tons) before arriving in France in August 1941.

The *Orion's* circumnavigation of the world had taken sixteen months. Her careful preparation had been worth the effort. She had not been challenged. The only time the New Zealand or Australian naval authorities knew her whereabouts was when the *Komet* radioed Sydney to have the prisoners taken off Emirau. She suffered only one casualty—a crew member killed by accident. Yet with her guns and torpedoes she had sunk, or helped sink, eleven ships for a total of almost 70 000 tons. And the minefield she laid at the entrance to Auckland Harbour was to account for three more ships.

Kurt Weyher was awarded a Knights Cross of the Iron Cross and was to survive the war, living into the 1980s. The *Orion* did not go to sea again as a raider. It was sunk by an air attack in May 1945.

* * *

On 18 June 1940 the *Niagara* sailed through the minefield and anchored in Auckland. Later that night it cast off and proceeded on its journey to Canada.

* * *

The German Y-type mine, of which the *Orion* had left 228 in the Hauraki Gulf, was a moored contact mine. That is, when put in the water its anchor would descend to the bottom and it would be moored by means of a pre-set wire to float beneath the surface. It had 'horns' protruding from it. Inside these horns were fragile glass tubes and inside these glass tubes was sulphuric acid. If a ship hit a mine with sufficient impact to bend one of the soft metal horns, then the glass tube would break. When this happened the sulphuric acid inside would run down to the bottom of the tube where it would surround a small carbon plate and a zinc plate. The result was a battery producing approximately 1.8 volts of current. The current passed through a thin platinum wire in fulminate of mercury. This was the last stage in the process, resulting in the detonation of the high explosive, amatol. The delay between the breaking of the glass and the detonation was between one and two seconds. This delay was desirable. A ship steaming towards a mine would usually hit it with the bow—the strongest part of any ship. As the ship would be moving, the moored mine would slide along its side, or underneath it. The delay in detonation meant the mine would explode against the side of the ship, where it would be more likely to blow a hole in the hull.

This is exactly what happened with the *Niagara*.

Able-Seaman Ray Nelson recalled:

It was somewhere in the vicinity of 2 o'clock in the morning. We'd left Auckland about midnight. We were just going up north of the Hen and Chickens [Islands] and just south of the Bay of Islands. I was pretty tired and I turned in that night. All I had on was this singlet, you know, no pants or anything. Anyway when this explosion went off we didn't know what it was at the time—whether it was a torpedo or a mine. We were sleeping in tiered bunks, you know, one bunk above the other. I was on a top bunk. When I woke up—I remember hitting the deck—the bunk that I was sleeping in was actually over the top of me. How it got there is anybody's guess. It was dark, we had no light, so I groped around in the dark and found a pair of trousers. I got out of the cabin as fast as possible. There was a lot of confusion naturally. There was quite a lot of damage to the fo'ard part of the ship. The number two hold had taken the blast of the explosion. The deck in that area was splintered. There were no hatches on any of the 'tween decks. When we left Sydney there was a large American car, something like a Chevrolet, on the hatches of the 'tween deck for transportation up to Vancouver. When I went past—when I went through the 'tween decks—I noticed you could see sky through where the hatches had been on the deck above. There were no beams and there was no car either. Whether it got shot straight out the hold, or whether it dropped back down again, I don't know, but it wasn't there.

Then I went to the bridge and Captain Martin sent me to try and find the ship's carpenter. One of his duties was to take soundings around the ship to see what sort of water we were carrying in the bilges. So he sent me to find the ships carpenter to take soundings to see if we were taking water in. Anyway I found him down at the 'tween decks close to number two hold. He had already dropped the sounding rod to take soundings there and he said, 'Jesus, the sounding rod has gone straight out through the bottom of the ship'.

That was directly over where the mine had hit. So anyway I went back up to the bridge and told the captain and he said, 'Go down into the fo'ard accommodation and close all the portholes.'

So I went down the fo'ard companionway and I got halfway down and suddenly I was up to my knees in water. I couldn't go any further. I reported that and by this time the ship was noticeably going down by the head and taking a list over to port. We'd done everything, like shutting the watertight doors along the bombed section. It was purely a question of was she going to stay afloat or was she going to sink? After a period of time had gone by it was clearly getting worse. All the lifeboats were ordered to be swung out and lowered to A-deck so that the passengers could board them. Captain Martin ordered to abandon ship. All the boats on the port side had very little difficulty in getting away because she was resting to port. The starboard side was higher than the port side. Most of the starboard side boats were away before the list became too steep. But we had trouble getting number one and number three boats away. They were the two most fo'ard lifeboats. My boat station was with the number one boat which was the captain's boat. This boat, by custom, is the last one away. We were lowering her down to get her away. We had to virtually skid her down the side of the ship the list had increased so much by then.

Sister H. Munroe, a nurse travelling on the *Niagara*, later wrote about the morning in the lifeboats:

The early morning was very dark, about 4.25 am. The lifeboats were gradually drifting apart all around the stricken *Niagara*. The great old ship seemed to have steadied, and the hope of all was that she would survive. At the end of half an hour the watertight bulkheads must have collapsed under the strain, for she slowly stood on end and slid under the surface. Sorrow was the predominant feeling for the passing of that fine old ship. We all felt we had lost a home. Even the men caught their breath as, like a great shadow in the night, she vanished from view. A member of the crew in our boat expressed all our feelings in the words, 'she's a grand old lady and she's dying gracefully, though she doesn't want to die'.

We all felt the cold intensely. Sunrise brought curiosity as to our surroundings and somewhat revitalised us. Some tried chewing ship's biscuits—a tough proposition. Others became upset by the motion of the small boats on the swell. All were ready for rescue as the hours dragged on with us drifting, apparently anywhere, just drifting.

Bill Reynolds, a resident in the nearest town of Whangarei was awakened by his father.

First my father was awakened by the Whangarei Police who had received communication from Auckland Police that there had been a sinking of the *Niagara* outside Whangarei Heads and we were asked to get moving way out to the scene of the disaster as quick as we could, which we did forthwith.

It took almost three hours to get there. We reported to HMNZS *Achilles* who indicated that the scene of the disaster from six miles north, 40 east from where we were and to proceed with all haste. Well we certainly proceeded with all haste. We travelled at almost full speed for about half an hour before we first saw the tops of the masts of the lifeboats. They all had masts and lug sails.

When we eventually got closer, there they were, on a beautiful clear flat calm morning. Seventeen of them at sea like a miniature regatta. All loaded with passengers and their life jackets on. Some of them looking very forlorn, some of them with very little in the way of clothing.

* * *

It was dawn on 19 June 1940. On the other side of the world the sun was setting on what was the previous day. While the passengers of the *Niagara* huddled in their blankets and waited for rescue, Winston Churchill got to his feet in the House of Commons and made one of his most famous speeches:

The Battle for France is over. I fear the Battle for Britain is about to begin. Upon this battle hangs the fate of Christian civilisation. Hitler knows he will have to break us in this island or lose the war. If we can stand up to him all Europe may be free and the life of the world may move forward into broad, sunlit uplands. But if we fail, then the whole world, including the United States of America, including all that we have known and cared for, will sink into an abyss of a new dark age, made more sinister, and perhaps more protracted, by the lights of perverted science. Let us therefore brace ourselves for our duties, and so bear ourselves that, if the British Empire and its Commonwealth last for a thousand years, men will still say, this was their finest hour.

With the sinking of the *Niagara* over eight tons of gold lay at the bottom of the sea. Gold belonging to England in what, history was to show, was indeed its finest hour.

The passengers and crew of the *Niagara*, all of whom survived the sinking, were rounded up in their lifeboats and transferred, first to the smaller faster ships that had come to rescue them, then to the RMS *Wanganella*. Aboard this ship they were taken back to Auckland where emergency accommodation was provided and arrangements made for their journey to resume.

* * *

In 1940 Australia's national banking interests were the responsibility of the Commonwealth Bank of Australia. As the Bank of a British Dominion the bank was 'answerable' to the Bank of England. To the Commonwealth Bank fell the task of informing the Bank of England that the *Niagara* had sunk. It did so with a cablegram that read: 'Boat carrying cargo referred to in our [cablegram] 85 reported sunk in Pacific. No details available yet'.

The next day the Bank of England replied saying: 'Admiralty here suggest enquiries should be made as to the possibility of salvage. Would you kindly consult Naval Authorities, Melbourne on this subject and let us have their views'.

The Naval Board in Melbourne then sent a telegram to its District Naval Offices around the country saying: '*Niagara* sunk in 60 fathoms. Request information whether there is diving equipment suitable for working at this depth available in Australia'.

The Naval Offices in each state then approached salvage firms, of which there were very few in Australia, to ask if they had a means of salvaging at this depth. Not surprisingly, almost all the responses were negative. Such equipment was unknown in Australia. And to both invent and manufacture it in a time of war would be, to say the least, a challenge.

Fortunately for the Bank of England, there was a man in Melbourne waiting for just such a challenge.

TWO

20 June – 9 December 1940

A Regular Millionaire's Yacht

John Protheroe Williams was born in Hull, England, in 1896. With the exception of a vague legend that their ancestors were Welsh pirates, the family was not a seafaring one. They were farmers and small landowners. Although they were not well-to-do, there was enough discipline and hard work within the family to ensure the boys went to a good school. At grammar school, unable to match the superior studying and retention powers of his older brother, John Williams read and dreamed away his time with stories like *Treasure Island* and *Westward Ho!*

When he failed the Junior Welsh Board examination, Williams' father admitted his second oldest son was no scholar and consented to allow the boy to go to sea. At fourteen years of age his father took him to the shipping office where he was registered as a seaman. He signed on a steamer, *King John*, bound for Port Said with a load of coal. On his first voyage Williams gained a desire to sail on the last of the tall ships.

Williams left the *King John* in 1914 and signed on the barque *Inverness*. It was during this voyage that the captain called them all aft and told them that England and Germany were at war. On two occasions during World War I Williams was to have sailing ships shot from under him by German U-boats. Submarines against sailing ships: World War I was a time of transition in the means and methods of seagoing warfare.

By 1920 square-rigged sailing ships had all but been replaced by steamers, but Williams had no taste for mechanical ships. There was no art in sailing them. Just constant noise and stink. In 1921 he sailed on a steamer to Australia where he met the woman who would become his wife and lost the desire for long ocean voyages. He worked steamers up and down the east coast, then got his first job ashore. One day while watching men unload bales using ropes he decided the job could be done more quickly, and with fewer men, by using hooks. As a result he started a stevedoring company and his fortunes began to prosper. He worked out faster ways of unloading coal, using mechanical grabs, and gained knowledge which he would later put to use on the *Niagara*.

When the Australian waterfronts were hit by long running and bitter strikes in the 1930s, Williams stood firmly on the side of the employers and made enemies in labour movement—enemies, time was to show, who had long memories. After the strikes the waterfront settled down to a period of relative harmony, and Williams to a period of prosperity. But in reading Williams own words, as well as other opinions about the man, one soon gets a feeling that settling down to anything was not in the nature of John Protheroe Williams. He craved more. Whether it was more work, more power, more social status, more knowledge or more challenges, the man's combination of restlessness, determination and ambition would constantly have him seeking some new activity. Thus in the 1930s he spread his interests into goldmining and started an engineering company. By 1940 he was prosperous, hard working, and still fiercely loyal to Great Britain.

Two weeks before World War II was declared, the 43-year-old Williams enlisted in the Australian Navy Reserve. If he thought his experience as a seaman and a leader of men would have him sailing the seas again and fighting Germans, he was wrong. He found himself in a small office doing paperwork. Then he was put in charge of collecting cannon out of public parks, where they had sat as monuments and playthings, and having them made operable again so they could be used on merchant ships. He felt he wasn't doing worthwhile work for the war effort and refused to collect his pay.

Finally he wrote to the Naval Board, saying that a schoolboy could be of more service to his country, and he was released from the Navy Reserve. Next he was appointed a captain in the army, with a view to specialising in transport. But this seemed to hold no more promise of worthwhile service. Later he recalled how he spent his days marching and doing sword drills.

But then the *Niagara* sank.

* * *

For diver John Edward Johnstone, 'Jack' to some and 'Johnno' to many, involvement with Captain Williams began not with the sinking of the *Niagara* but, coincidentally, with the sinking of another Union Steam Ship Company vessel almost four years earlier. On the night of 29 January 1937 a small coastal trader, the *Kakariki* was steaming towards the Port of Melbourne. Another ship, the *Caradale*, had just steamed down the river and entered the bay. In circumstances that both captains disputed, the *Caradale* sliced into the side of the *Kakariki* which sank in shallow water, its funnel and masts still visible. Johnstone was called out of his bed at 4 a.m. and asked to go to the wreck to recover five bodies still missing. This he did, and later became interested in the idea of refloating the *Kakariki*. He wrote:

The matter of the salvage and refloating the vessel interested me. I had gone into this pretty thoroughly. The damaged bow plating could be cut away and with the watertight bulkhead between the two holds, the rest could have been floated. First thing that would have to be done would be to discharge the pyrites to lighten the ship. With this in mind I got in touch with J. P. Williams, who was then manager of a ship stevedoring company. Together we went into the salvage, him to discharge the cargo and me to take over the underwater work.

Tenders were called for and this led to the United Salvage Company. He and I were to be joint partners. We tendered without success. The *Kakariki* remained where it sank.

The first business dealing between Williams and Johnstone also marked their first misunderstanding. If Johnstone felt, as he later wrote, that they were partners in the salvage bid, it was not apparent to Williams. As a result of the *Kakariki*, Williams became interested in salvage as a business venture. A year after it sank he wrote to the

Melbourne Harbour Trust on United Stevedoring Pty Ltd letterhead:

Dear Sirs,

    The above company, or a subsidiary to be formed by them, contemplates making an effort to salvage the s.s. Kakariki, and requests your permission should she be lifted clear of the bottom to tow her to the westward and beach her in an area to be agreed upon . . .

    Although Williams wasn't given the opportunity to refloat the *Kakariki*, he continued to pursue his interest in the idea of salvage as a business. On 29 April 1939 the United Salvage Proprietary Limited was incorporated under the *Companies Act*. It had four shareholders. Johnstone was not one of them. Yet his writing of that period still gives the impression that he felt he was a partner in Williams' salvage venture:

Two years went by and we had done a few jobs as such and more or less had become known in shipping circles. The day the phone call by Captain Williams for me to 'drop everything and come right over' convinced me we had the *Kakariki* salvage contract.

    'Let us forget the *Kakariki*, Johnno', said Williams.

    This is very confidential. You have read of the loss of the RMS *Niagara* off the New Zealand coast. She has two and a half million pounds worth of gold bars in the bullion room and I have been asked if our company would be interested.

    *   *   *

For John Protheroe Williams, the sinking of the *Niagara* was an opportunity to do something important for his country and the British Commonwealth, something that had never been done before. A far cry from removing cannon from public parks and making them operable again, it was an opportunity he seized with both hands. Eight tons of British gold sat at the bottom of the sea, probably deeper than anyone had salvaged before. Over the coming weeks he did everything possible to be given the job and convince people that he could do it.

    He flew to New Zealand, chartered a ship from the Auckland Harbour Board and went to the area of the wreck. Using an echo sounder he explored the seabed. This he found to be generally flat at a depth of 360 feet (60 fathoms). However, at one point the echo sounder 'showed an object rising approximately 120 feet from the bottom and 500 feet in length'. The *Niagara* was 522 feet long and if it was sitting on its keel the funnels would reach over 130 feet in height. Williams was confident he had found the wreck.

On his return to Australia he submitted a ten page report to the Commonwealth Bank, in which he spoke optimistically about the chances for success. The salvage, Williams estimated, would take approximately six months and cost the bank £27 800. The report concluded:

In the course of the Report we have suggested not only that an attempt at salvage is well worth while, but that the chances of success are good, provided the vessel is upright and substantially undamaged . . . and finally, that our opinion of the prospects is sufficiently high to cause us to offer to contribute gear and services to the value of some thousands of pounds on the basis that no charge will be made should success not attend to our efforts.

The Royal Australian Navy had approached all known salvage companies. Only Williams and one other claimed to have equipment capable at working at such a depth. The other had an experimental diving suit which the Australian Navy had tested and found not workable. The only real possibility was Williams, and he had certainly demonstrated his eagerness for the job. The Commonwealth Bank saw no alternative but to give it to him. It made discreet enquiries into his character and, finding him to be 'capable, keen and resourceful', recommended him to the Bank of England. The Bank of England, in response to this information, cabled the Commonwealth Bank of Australia saying: 'Should be grateful therefore if you will contact Williams with a view to obtaining details as to when operations could begin . . . and the general terms of contract to be entered into.'

The 'general terms' of the contract were that United Salvage would pay for the design and manufacture of its own salvage gear, while the Bank of England would pay the wages of Williams and the crew plus the expenses of the salvage, including hire of a suitable ship and operating costs. The total of these expenses would be no more than £30 000 sterling. In the event that gold was recovered, United Salvage Pty Ltd would receive 2.5 per cent of its value.

At this point the question raised is whether the salvage attempt was an 'official' job undertaken on behalf of the government in a time of war, or whether it was a private contractual salvage undertaken for profit. If it was purely a government job, done by men in wartime for their country, then no percentage would be payable. The risks and dangers would be undertaken for King and country. Like any enlisted men, they would receive their pay and put their lives at risk without any claim of further reward.

If on the other hand it was a private salvage, undertaken for profit, then 2.5 per cent was ludicrously low. Salvage contracts quite often call for 50 per cent to go to the salvors. Where no contract exists, such as when a seaman acts 'beyond the call of duty' to save a sinking ship, the generally agreed-upon figure is one-third. In this case there was, with one questionable exception, no one else willing to undertake the job. Few people thought it even possible. It could be termed 'extremely high risk' and in such cases salvors would normally ask for 50 per cent.

Williams faced a dilemma. He wanted to do something for his country in the war. Salvaging the gold was his opportunity. He wanted his own men and be in charge himself. But he had other shareholders in United Salvage who were businessmen and while Williams was satisfied with this contract the other shareholders appear to have felt that 2.5 per cent was not enough, especially if they were to be taxed on the profit. They argued for at least double that amount.

On 3 September 1940, G. M. Shain, who was the bank's representative in Melbourne, negotiating with Williams, wrote to Sir Harry Sheehan, Governor of the Commonwealth Bank of Australia, saying:

I went to Flinders Naval Base today and had a long conference with Captain Williams. The terms enumerated in your letter were conveyed to him and he will take the matter up with his fellow Directors immediately, and hoped to be able to advise me of their reactions in the course of a few days time. He gave me the impression that at least one of his fellow Directors may attempt to make a better bargain of the salvage and again hinted to me that should they be too grasping, it might be desirable for the matter to be undertaken by the Australian Navy and his services co-opted for the work. In that event he has no doubt that his personnel from the United Salvage Co. could be co-opted also.

Captain Williams himself is quite satisfied in the tentative terms offered.

Williams managed to convince his fellow shareholders to accept the 2.5 per cent and therefore didn't need to have his services 'co-opted' to the Navy. With assistance from the Commonwealth Bank he worked out an agreement with the Australian government whereby the 2.5 per cent would not be taxed—an agreement that was later disputed. Williams' fellow shareholders were still not absolutely certain, but the contract was signed on 2 October 1940. Williams was the only one to sign his name as an individual. The other shareholders signed on behalf of their companies, cautious that, if they were taxed, then the tax payable by their companies would be less than that payable by them as individuals. As a consequence the contract was no longer with a single company, but with three companies and an individual. This group was then referred to as the United Salvage Syndicate.

But Williams had his contract. More importantly, he had his 'impossible job'. He could now do something that would make the world take note and his first step was to find a way to work at depths of up to 600 feet underwater.

*   *   *

The underwater observation chamber that Williams had built now stands in the Market Museum in the small country town of Castlemaine, Victoria. When its active life was over it was returned to the community that built it. An open, spacious building, the Market Museum houses old photographs, kerosene lamps, swords, medals, old furniture, horse-drawn wagons and the other things one usually finds in museums in Australian country towns. The exception in this case is the chamber. It stands nine feet six inches tall, weighs over two tons and looks like something out of a Jules Verne novel. Because of its size and weight it originally stood on the street in front of the old market building. But after vandals started writing graffiti on it a hole was cut in the wooden floor of the museum, a concrete slab poured and the chamber brought inside. Beside the chamber are six photographs of the salvage and a short caption that briefly explains the details.

In 1940, methods of working underwater below 200 feet were virtually unknown. Over 100 years earlier the 'full diving dress' had been invented. This was basically a copper helmet attached to a canvas suit. With lead-soled shoes and air hoses to the surface the diver could, in a clumsy fashion, walk around the seabed while air was pumped down to him from the surface.

Such full-dress diving suits were only practical to a depth of 200 feet. In such flexible suits, where the water exerts pressure on the diver's body, compressed air must be breathed to stop the lungs being crushed. Breathing air which is increasingly compressed creates its own problems, as air under pressure becomes liquid and nitrogen bubbles form in the bloodstream. Diving tables of this period showed a diver could work at a depth of 200 feet for ten minutes and then spend thirty minutes decompressing while coming to the surface. But 200 feet was a long way short of the estimated depth in which the *Niagara* had sunk. Later mixed gas breathing would allow divers to descend deeper in flexible suits, but that science was in its infancy in 1940 and unknown in Australia.

The only way to lower a man to somewhere between 350 and 600 feet would be to seal him inside a solid chamber that protected his body from the water pressure. This meant that air could not be pumped down to him from the surface. Nor could he get out of the chamber underwater or operate or move anything outside. He could only be sealed inside and the whole chamber lowered on a rope or wire. The diver, or more correctly, the observer, could look out the windows or portholes, then by means of a telephone line to the surface, report what he could see. The men in the salvage vessel above would lower hooks and grabs and, working blind, move these up and down, left and right, according to the instructions, trying to move or lift what they wanted. It was a slow and clumsy method of working.

This method of salvage had been used once before. With a German-made observation chamber, Italians had salvaged gold from the *Egypt* lying in 420 feet of water off the coast of France. But as Germany and Italy were now enemies there would be no chance of Williams getting information or technical assistance from them. Williams did have one source of information however. An English journalist, David Scott, had accompanied the Italians on their salvage and had written a book called *Egypt's Gold*, which contained photographs of the observation chamber. Fortunately Williams had a copy. He read it, then approached a Melbourne engineer, David V. Isaacs, to design such a chamber.

Among Williams' original instructions, which he wrote to Isaacs, were the following considerations:

The main consideration in the construction of this Chamber, is that it should be made without any projections which tend towards fouling, having in mind that it may well be necessary for the occupant to be lowered through apertures blasted in the various decks of the steamer from which the material is to be salvaged.

Consideration must be given to the possibility of the hoisting rope becoming severed, in which case, the Diver must have the opportunity of so increasing his buoyancy that he should float to the surface.

Isaacs designed the chamber on what he described as 'pure engineering principals'. The body was made from half inch thick mild steel, rolled and welded at the joint to form a cylinder 52 inches high and just over three feet in diameter. The dome on top of the cylinder was cast from manganese bronze five eighths of an inch thick. Both components were made at the Thompsons Engineering and Pipe Co Ltd at Castlemaine, then bolted together.

Once the diver was inside the chamber there was no way he could escape from it until someone outside undid the four stainless steel bolts that held the lid. Three mechanisms were incorporated into the design to assist the diver to bring the whole chamber to the surface should the suspending wire become entangled or severed. The first was release of the suspending wire. The diver did this by unscrewing three bolts above his head which held the chains outside attached to the suspending wire. Second, unscrewing bolts beneath his feet the diver could release one or both of the 300 pound weights that were attached underneath the chamber. And around the rim of the bottom of the chamber was a ballast tank. This would normally be filled with water, but in an emergency the diver could force compressed oxygen into the tank, blow out the water and so increase the buoyancy.

On dry land (or on the deck of a ship) the observation chamber weighed 4 710 pounds (or 2.1 tons). The gravitational pull of an object decreases underwater. Once submerged the chamber 'weighed' 300 pounds. With air blown into the ballast tank it had positive buoyancy of 150 pounds. That is, the gravitational pull was 'reversed' and the chamber tried to float to the surface with a pull of 150 pounds. With air in the ballast tank and both weights dropped from the bottom the positive buoyancy was 600 pounds.

Inside the chamber the diver was totally sealed off. He could breathe the air for a short time but this quickly became stale. The diver wore a mask which fitted over his mouth and nose so his exhaled air passed through a tube and entered a container of soda lime which absorbed the carbon dioxide. A cylinder containing 40 cubic feet of compressed oxygen was carried inside the chamber and the diver would periodically release oxygen. Thus he breathed the same air over and over again, replenishing the oxygen and having his carbon dioxide absorbed by chemicals.

By this means he could stay in the chamber for ten hours.

The 'theory of elastic stability' as published in 1936, was known to Isaacs and he could design both the upper manganese bronze dome and the lower mild steel cylinder of the chamber on known principles. He therefore designed these components to withstand 270 pounds per square inch, or a depth of 600 feet.

Less was known about the properties of glass under pressure. There was no armoured glass available in Australia, only standard plate glass used in windows and Isaacs began having this tested to see what would be required and at what depth it would be safe. He was not able to reach a definitive conclusion. The one and a quarter

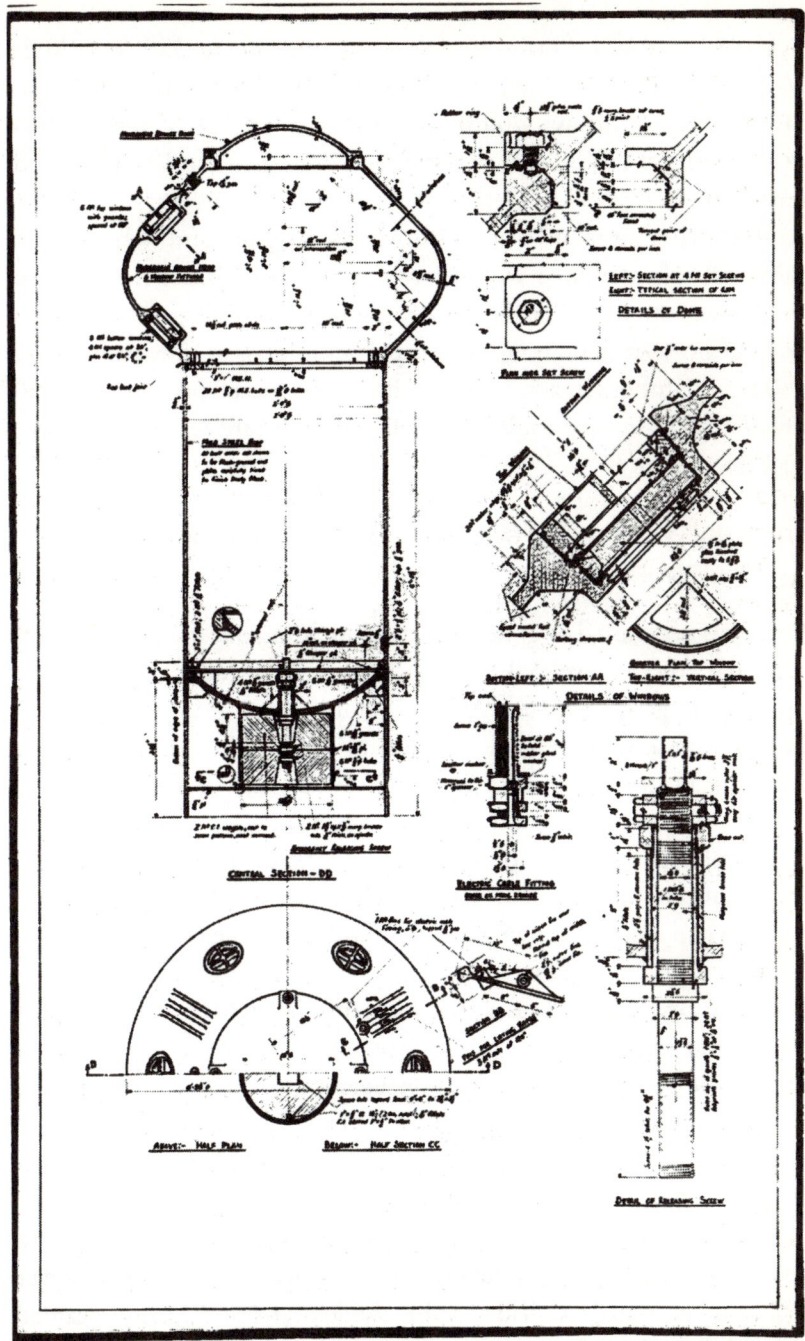

The blueprint for the underwater observation chamber designed by David Isaacs.

inch glass in the windows he felt would be safe to 350 feet. After Williams' reported that this was the approximate depth, Isaacs was confident the windows would not break, but wrote that 'if the depth were increased to 450 feet the stresses in the glass [are] to my mind getting fairly high'.

The other area of uncertainty was fatigue, and what affect continual submergence would have on the glass. Isaacs noted, 'The only point I am in doubt about now is whether my alleged authorities really know as much about the properties of glass as they profess to'.

The chamber, Isaacs concluded, would resist pressure to 600 feet. The glass in the windows he felt would be safe to 350 feet. After that, no one knew . . .

*   *   *

While the chamber was being built Williams chose a crew. He later described its formation:

A crew? Who wanted to go to a special ship fitting out in New Zealand? Just about everyone we spoke to. Alf Warren a diver for us pre-war along with Johnstone. A Londoner, Alf, brought up in an orphanage. A diver on the Dover Breakwater for Sir Wm. Arrol in 1906. Wrecked on the Goodwin Sands in a brig, of all things, before that. Silent, near six feet tall, lightly though well built. Steady and courageous to a fault.

Bill Johnstone (brother of John) was a navy diver and a shipwright. As good a diver as the other but stable, disciplined, cheerful always with no malice in him. Bill, as a shipwright, and Alf with an engine driver's certificate, knew their stuff and did it.

Arthur Bryant. Steady as a rock and dependable. More religious than the rest and prepared to stick to his principles. Quietly spoken and well behaved. No job too disagreeable or dangerous.

Billy Green was my car driver. Why did I take him? Because he wanted to go and was young and active, with a ton of guts. He justified himself from the day he joined.

To look after the food business? Stan Mitchell. Not only a first rate steward but a kindly gentle fellow. The very man for such a job. Never really put out, Stan. If we had been his children, and surely he so regarded us, he couldn't have done more.

Our boatswain: Daniel Scott. Sailor, blacksmith par excellence, a first-class rigger, a steeplejack he had been at one time. Tattooed all over—hands and feet and all. Hailing from Northern Ireland, the Orange part, he did his piece throughout.

Then Joe Alcock, another North of Ireland man, a sailor and a fisherman, sick with ulcers and badly; but ulcers or not he stuck it out like a Briton.

With the exception of Bill Johnstone, the crew that Williams picked had worked for him previously. Bill Johnstone was given six months 'leave without pay' from the Royal Australian Navy to join his diver brother. It was a diverse group of men. Alf Warren, tall and silent and already over 70 years of age. The heavy drinking Danny Scott. Joe Alcock sick with ulcers. Arthur Bryant, 25 years of age, quiet, religious and engaged to be married. Young Billy Green. The Johnstone brothers. And two others who were never later mentioned. John Thompson and Max Paulson. A mixed crew of English, Irish, Canadian and Australian.

Williams left for New Zealand on 18 October 1940. Johnstone and the rest of the crew would stay in Australia until the chamber was finished. Williams' task was to try to find a suitable salvage vessel. To assist him, the bank had arranged for him to carry a personal letter of introduction from the Australian Prime Minister, Robert Menzies, which read:

This will serve to introduce you to Captain John Protheroe Williams of South Melbourne, Victoria who is proceeding to the Dominion of New Zealand in connection with the salvage operations of S.S. 'Niagara'.

Any courtesies or facilities that may be extended to Captain Williams during his stay will be greatly appreciated.

Yours faithfully,
R. G. Menzies.
Prime Minister.

'Captain Williams told me', Arthur Bryant recalled, 'before he left for New Zealand, the Prime Minister had said [to him], "succeed in this and you and those under you may have any honour you like to name"'.

* * *

Arriving in Auckland, Williams immediately began looking for a salvage ship, but everything that was suitable was beyond his limited budget. Finally someone told him about a derelict coastal steamer lying on the mud on the far side of Auckland Harbour. He wrote:

Seeing nothing else I thought I might as well have a look at her anyhow. So I hired a boat and went across. A wreck, at first sight. Rust everywhere—doors gone, portholes stolen, no steering gear, no telegraph. Seabirds' eggs on top of the cylinders of her little reciprocating engine.

I went over and over and around her most of the day. I sat on her shambles of a foredeck and pondered over her. Went down into her little saloon with its few passenger rooms leading off and then wandered about her deck again, with the idiotic refrain running in my head . . . 'Will she, won't she? Will she, won't she? Won't she join the dance?'

Finally I made up my mind to give the old girl a go.

The *Claymore*, a good name.

The *Claymore* was owned by the New Zealand government. There were plans to use it as a hulk as part of the boom defence of Auckland Harbour, but Williams was able to hire the *Claymore* for £250 for six months. It was refloated, then towed to Seagers Shipbuilding Yard where the work of rebuilding her commenced. Derricks and spars were fitted, decks repaired, the portholes (the brass and glass from which had long since been stolen) were blanked off, rivet holes were filled, larger holes were covered with steel plates, a new rudder was made, all valves were dismantled and cleaned, boiler mountings were replaced, the water tank was drained and lined with cement, the boiler was cleaned and loads of bricks, dirt and rubbish were removed and a new bridge built. The propeller, which had one blade missing, was not replaced.

Williams also had the job of equipping the *Claymore*. Cables, chains, buoys, life-saving gear, a galley stove, anchors, tarpaulins, ropes—in fact just about everything other than the hull and engines had to be replaced. Williams went to anyone he could and asked to borrow equipment with a promise that it would be returned at the end of the salvage. Sometimes people were agreeable, sometimes they were not. An insight into the 'scavenging' and to Williams himself is provided in the notes he kept during these weeks of fitting out:

Thursday November 7th, 1940. Saw both Burns and Co and Foster and put it on them to loan me all the boat gear on some basis of payment on a valuation at the end of the job. I may manage this though it savours more than a little of effrontery to say the least of it, but I don't care who goes down on this job so long as the Bank of England comes out on top and I am quite prepared to resort to anything to gain that end.

Another reference in Williams' notes, as he prepared the *Claymore* for sea, mentions Sir Ernest Davis, the Mayor of Auckland. It is not a complimentary reference:

During the evening, having slept all the afternoon, was introduced to the great Ted Theodore by Sir Ernest Davis. Found him a pleasant fellow, Theodore I mean, Davis as usual weighing in with a lot of silly suggestions but closed up like an oyster when I suggested that he should hire me the junk out of his yard on the basis of a valuation and then a percentage of it when it was returned.

As Williams wrote this he was not to know that, in Australia a second group were making plans to salvage the gold from the *Niagara*. Nor was he to know that they continually received accurate information on the progress and movements of the *Claymore*. Williams may have attributed the reluctance of Sir Ernest Davis to provide him with materials as selfishness. He would have been interested to learn that one of the men in the salvage group making preparations in Sydney, one Sidney Hyam Davis, was Sir Ernest's nephew.

It was during this time that Williams was joined by the first of the New Zealand crew members. Ray Nelson had been an ableseaman on the *Niagara* when it sank. He was the second *Claymore* crew member I was to find still living and he told me how he came to join the crew.

After the *Niagara* sank I joined a collier which was running from the South Island to Auckland. On the grapevine I heard that there was a captain in Auckland, came over from Australia, looking at salvaging the gold. Anyway I found out who he was and where he stayed and I went round to see him. I introduced myself and told him that I was a member of the crew of the *Niagara* and that if he was going to make an attempt to salvage the gold I wanted to be with him. Anyway he said, 'that's great, just keep in touch' and subsequently I joined the crew'.

While Williams haggled and scrounged to get the *Claymore* ready, his crew in Australia were preparing to follow him to New Zealand. Williams was careful not to let them know the condition of the ship. Johnstone received a letter from him telling of his 'find'. 'The very thing for a salvage ship. Even with a saloon and cabins. Wants a little doing up but this will be no problem'.

Johnstone wrote:

My brother found a cutting from an old newspaper where it [the *Claymore*] was described. She had been built in Scotland as long ago as 1902, but her description made her sound wonderful. She was 115 feet long and had been the pride of New Zealand shipping, with luxurious saloons and cabins panelled in walnut and with electricity throughout. A regular millionaire's yacht! We were all delighted.

The crew sailed from Sydney on 15 November, taking with them the observation chamber secretly stowed in the hold. Six days later Williams led them down to the wharf to see their 'millionaire's yacht'. Johnstone wrote:

... when we saw her we could only stand and gaze in horror. Not this wreck surely? The skipper had not told us he had found the *Claymore* lying in the mud where she had been retired to years before, and that what had not been stripped out of her when she was laid up had long since been looted. She looked a complete wreck as she leaned against the coal hulk where she was berthed, rusted, what paint she had long since gone, her masts and deckhouses splattered and streaked with bird mess. The decks, when we got on board, sprouted slimy grass and weed, and birds had nested everywhere. Inside, in the cabins and saloons, she stank of damp mould, stagnant pools of rain water that had come through her rotted deck planks, and rats. We were to find rats everywhere.

Johnstone was also faced with another concern. He wrote:

...I was not aware that Williams had formed the United Salvage Syndicate. Besides himself were four others. Williams asked me what I would expect to get out of it, in the event of success. I asked for £5 000 and a retainer of £80 a month.

The day of our departure . . . I was asked to sign the contract. Instead of £5 000 it was £3 000 on a pro-rata arrangement on two million pounds recovery. Over and above the two million, I would not benefit. I took exception to this and discussed the clause with Williams and I quote him. 'Rather late to bring this up as it is what the Syndicate have agreed on. It has been a job to get them into it. Any hitch now and they will pull out. I will tell you what I'll do with you. Whatever I get and whatever you get, we will pool and go 50/50', said Williams.

I agreed to this and we shook hands on it. A gentleman's agreement and I trusted Williams implicitly. My brother had no agreement with the Syndicate except on a retainer of £10 a week. I was to share with him what came of the 50/50 pool with Williams.

On 19 November, Williams began a logbook for the *Claymore* in which he would write daily for the next year. Personal comments are almost non-existent in this logbook, but on 9 December 1940, with crew aboard, his observation chamber stowed and his salvage vessel ready to take on the impossible, he allowed himself a short but proud observation: 'It's 12 minutes to 4. The old tub moves away, no longer "S.S. Claypit" but "Salvage Vessel Claymore". Vessel's preparation for sea finalised'.

For the first time in eleven years—and for what would be the last time—the *Claymore* steamed out of Auckland Harbour and headed for the coastal town of Whangarei.

On the 100 mile trip north its engine broke down four times.

THREE

10 December 1940 – 16 January 1941

When a Beggar He Prepares to Plunge

My first trip to Whangarei was with my wife, Zoe, and two friends who had volunteered to work as a television crew and paid their own air fares to New Zealand to do so.

It was a year after Danny Scott had died in an old person's home and Arthur Bryant had written his letter to the editor of *Australasian Post*. In that time Zoe and I had found four crew members of the *Claymore* who were still alive. We'd spent days, sometimes weeks, searching archives for official records of the salvage, and months tracking down the families of the crew members.

We had also learned that John Johnstone had taken his 16 mm movie camera with him on the salvage job and filmed the entire event. I now had that film and hoped to combine it with interviews of the crew and the people who helped them to make a television documentary. Thinking there might be people in Whangarei who still remembered the salvage, I had placed a press release in the local paper and received over twenty letters in response. It was to record some interviews that we first went to Whangarei.

One of the people we spoke to was 84-year-old Mary Sanson. Over 50 years earlier she had worked in the Whangarei Harbour Master's Office as a secretary. She recalled Captain Williams' arrival in the town:

Well he just arrived at the Whangarei Harbour Board Office and enquired whether he could see our Harbour Master and our Harbour Master at the time was out, as he often was and I think Captain Williams was rather taken aback. What I said was, 'Well he isn't in at the moment. You will probably find him at the pub up at the corner of the road.

Well he glared at me. I suppose well trained office girls didn't give their bosses away like that.

Williams eventually rented a house in Whangarei and his wife and three young children came from Australia and joined him. The rest of the crew, including divers John and Bill Johnstone, were accommodated on the *Claymore*.

Sleeping arrangements on board were not ideal. Bill Johnstone put a sheet of corrugated iron over his bunk to stop water dripping on him when he slept. Others often repeated tales of waking to find rats running over their face. And sea water flowed through the cabins. But the crew soon made friends with the townspeople and when ashore were often taken to their homes where they could sleep in a dry bed, eat a hearty meal and spend a welcome evening by a warm fire.

For the first two days after the *Claymore* arrived in Whangarei the crew were occupied making her ready to begin the search. While he waited for a minesweeper to arrive, Williams wrote a letter to G. M. Shain, the Commonwealth Bank's representative in Melbourne:

At the moment I am more than a little concerned about the attitude of the Superintendent of the Naval Base in Auckland with regard to the sweeping of the area in which we are about to start work . . . when I first arrived [in New Zealand] I advised him I anticipated being ready about December 1st and he undertook to have the minesweeping done long before that date. When the *Claymore* passed the survey I again took the matter up and received the same answer. Three weeks ago I interviewed Commander Bingley once more on the subject and was told the sweepers were to go within a few days. At the beginning of this week I saw him again and asked whether it had been done and I received the answer that the matter had escaped his attention.

I may say that in my last interview with Bingley in order to get some action, I said that I would start when I got ready, whether the place was swept or not. Later on the same day he telephoned me to say the War Council forbade me to go to the area but whether this is true or has been said to cover the thing up I do not know.

On 14 December the minesweepers *Duchess* and *South Sea* swept an area approximately one mile around the position where the *Niagara* was believed to have sunk. This area was the one in which Williams, on his earlier trip to New Zealand, by means of an echo sounder, had found an object rising 120 feet from the seabed. They also swept a 'track' half a mile wide to the Whangarei Heads, so that the *Claymore* could safely reach the area.

The minesweepers returned to Auckland. Williams started dragging this area with a trawl wire in an attempt to hook the *Niagara*, but without success. The object 'rising from the seabed' was not the *Niagara*, but simply a natural underwater formation. The search area would have to be widened. Williams did not inform the navy of this.

The *Claymore* returned to Whangarei for water and supplies, then proceeded to sea again on Christmas Day.

The crew practised lowering the chamber over the side. On deck a special derrick was needed to lift it out of the forward hold and swing it over the side. Once partly submerged it weighed less, and a crew member would climb on the top and hitch it to a lighter, more manoeuvrable derrick. Lifting the chamber in and out of the water was not an easy task. If there was a swell, with the *Claymore* rising and falling, the chamber often bobbed and jumped when it was partly submerged.

On 29 December, with the weather calm, Williams decided to lower the observation chamber to the bottom to test it. It still had not been submerged lower than the surface of the water, so it was not known if the windows could withstand the pressure. First the chamber was sent down loaded with sandbags. It returned to the surface with none of the glass windows broken; the depth gauge showed 500 feet and the interior was dry.

John Johnstone got into the chamber and the lid was bolted down. He recorded the details in the notebook he carried with him:

In bell 11.32. Oxy flow on oxygen 5 lbs. Barometer 2.5 lbs. Lift from hold [of *Claymore*] 11.40 a.m. Entered water 11.42 a.m.

Reading on gauge 11.46 at 60 feet. Good light.
11.47 20 fathoms
11.48 25 fathoms

WHEN A BEGGAR HE PREPARES TO PLUNGE

11.49 35 fathoms

At 11.55 a.m. he recorded he reached the bottom at 61 fathoms, then made notes of what he could see:

Mud bottom. Cloud created by rolling of cylinder in mud. Fish quite visible to 10 feet. Total darkness in bell. Desirable light be carried for reading of gauges.

Gauge crept to 61.5 fathoms . . . looking on bottom is like floating on clouds owing to soft mud.

Johnstone continued making observations until the chamber left the bottom 23 minutes later.

12.20 50 fathoms
12.22 45 fathoms
12.23 40 fathoms
12.25 35 fathoms
12.26 30 fathoms
Wire rope in port window
12.26 25 fathoms
Wire rope 12 feet away.

'Suddenly I heard another sound', Johnstone later wrote. 'Not on the telephone but against the bell'.

Johnstone called up to Williams to stop raising the chamber.

'Then I saw what caused the scraping sound I heard. The bell had fouled a wire rope that I could see pressing against one of my glass windows'.

Johnstone asked Williams to see if there were any wires hanging over the side of the *Claymore*. There were not. 'I examined the wire', Johnstone wrote:

It was not round like our wires, but square, the corners serrated like the blade of a hacksaw. And suddenly I remembered. This [wire] was not from the ship but from the sea bottom, the mooring wire of a German mine. These moorings were serrated like this to cut through a minesweeper's trawling wire. The bell was fastened to enough high explosive to blow me and the *Claymore* sky high if it exploded.

I heard the skipper calling me [through the telephone] telling me there was no wire hanging over the ship's side and that he was taking me up. I tried not to show how I was feeling as I told him not to heave me up. I dared not tell him what I had found and my brain was working fast trying to think how I could get clear of this danger. I could see from how the wire hung that it was around the bell.

Over the telephone in the observation chamber Johnstone told Williams aboard the *Claymore*, to heave up very slowly:

It was agony waiting. Hearing the wire scraping against the bell as it was raised. I peered out of my windows, waiting for disaster. Anyhow it would be a quick end. I would not even hear the explosion.

I was watching the wire, hands over my ears in an instinctive if futile protection. I saw the dark bulk of the mine, the shackle where the wire was secured close to my face. The bell was rising, slowly, and then, scarcely daring to breathe, I saw the mine sway in front of me and drift away slowly. It passed downward, seeming huge and like some lazy, moving animal, then it was gone and I heard the cry, 'bell in sight' on my phones.

I was sweating and shaking.

Through sheer good luck the mine had cleared itself as the observation chamber was raised slowly. At 12.33 p.m., exactly one hour after the lid had been bolted down and Johnstone sealed inside, the four bolts were undone and Johnstone lifted out. Away from the rest of the crew he told Williams what he had found. It was decided to heave up the anchor and move to another area.

The crew were still not aware that the chamber had been foul of a mine. At 2.30 p.m. they began to haul up the anchor. Ray Nelson recalled what happened.

Danny Scott was up on the bow waiting for the anchor to come in and he said 'There's something here'. Someone else looked over and said 'Well I think it might be a sunfish'. Danny said 'Nah, I think it's a cloud of mud, coming off the anchor, clouding the water'.

Anyway he gave signals to heave it up slowly and as it came closer it was quite obviously a mine covered in sort of cabbage and weed, but you could distinctly see the prongs sticking out.

The mine that had fouled the observation chamber was now fouled on the anchor line.

At this point Bill Johnstone was dressed in his standard diving dress and lowered over the side of the *Claymore* to inspect the mine under the water. He reported the anchor wire was wrapped around the mine. The *Claymore* had spent the previous night at anchor, and as it drifted around with the changing tides, it had wrapped itself around the mine wire.

The most obvious way to avoid the danger of the mine would simply be to cut the anchor line and steam away. But when a ship lies at anchor, the line to the anchor does not go directly down to the seabed. The length of the anchor line may be four times or more the depth of the water. To dig into the seabed and so not be dragged, an anchor needs to lie flat. To assist it, a length of chain or cable usually joins the anchor to the anchor line. Lighter rope is used closer to the surface so it is easier to manage. The *Claymore*'s anchor line at this point consisted of (as well as the anchor) 1 200 feet of wire, 240 feet of cable and a coil of three and a half inch manila rope. Williams was not only aware of the cost of replacing these items, but he was also aware that another anchor was not available in Whangarei.

The top of the anchor line was attached to a floating buoy. The *Claymore* would return to Whangarei, alert the Navy and return in two days time to try and separate the mine from the anchor and line. At 8.30 p.m. the *Claymore* sheltered in Urquharts Bay. The next morning Williams advised the Navy that they had found a mine.

On New Year's Day, 1941, the *Claymore* proceeded to sea. At 7 p.m. it made a rendezvous with HMNZS Minesweeper *Humphrey*, commanded by Lieutenant Neilson. Williams and John Johnstone went on board the minesweeper and explained the situation. The two ships waited out the night, then proceeded the next morning to where the buoy was attached to the anchor line and the mine.

The plan was to have the *Claymore* take hold of the buoy and lift the anchor line so the mine came close to the surface. While the line was held, John Johnstone in his diving suit would dive to the mine and shackle a line to the U-shaped holding point underneath it. This line would go to the *Humphrey*. With the anchor line to the *Claymore* and the newly attached mine line to the *Humphrey* the two ships would then steam in opposite directions and the mine would rise to the surface. It was hoped the mine's anchor line, which had been observed to be frayed, would break with the strain and the mine pop free of the *Claymore's* anchor. From here it would be unnecessary to explode it. Instead the Navy would simply shoot a hole in its casing, flooding the air chamber that kept it afloat, and the mine would sink to the bottom. Thus the *Claymore* would keep its precious anchor, chain and line.

That, at least, was the theory.

Firstly, all but the essential crew were taken from the *Claymore* and put on board the *Humphrey*. Remaining on board were Williams and John Johnstone, along with Arthur Bryant, Alf Warren, Danny Scott, Max Paulson and John Thompson.

With the majority of the crew clear, the *Claymore* hooked the buoy and steamed astern, pulling back on its anchor line in an attempt to bring the mine to the surface. The entry in the *Claymore's* logbook reads: '8.40 [a.m.] Buoy picked up and commenced heaving ... 8.53 [a.m.] Mine sighted attached to moorings six feet under vessel's hull.'

The *Claymore* stopped steaming astern and slacked off the line. In trying to bring the mine to the surface it was actually bringing it up under its own hull.

At this point it was decided to leave the mine where it was. John Johnstone and a diving party would get into the whaleboat, then diving just clear of the *Claymore*, he would attempt to shackle a line to the mine.

Williams, Johnstone, Arthur Bryant and John Thompson got into the whaleboat. Thompson became nervous and refused to continue. He was transferred to the minesweeper.

Now Johnstone got into his diving suit and prepared to take the line down to the mine. Strapped to each of his feet were lead-soled boots. On his chest and back were further lead weights. He was attached to the whaleboat by means of an air hose and a safety rope. The two were intertwined forming a kind of umbilical cord which did not go direct to his helmet, but was wound around his body so that he could tug on it more easily. Air was pumped to him from a compressor on the whaleboat.

To guide him, he would have a shot line—a thin rope with a weight on the end—lowered from the boat. In such a suit it was impossible for a man to swim. If he was going to work without the seabed under him, then the only way he could raise and lower himself was by inflating and deflating his suit. He ascended and descended as if he was inside a balloon. And to guide him up and down he used the shot line.

It is a cumbersome way for a man to dive but Johnstone was a master of it. Now his face plate was screwed into position and he heard the steady hiss of air as it was pumped to him. Via a small microphone and speaker in his helmet he could talk to his 'tenders' on the whaleboat, paying out or taking up the air line.

The last thing Williams said to him was, 'I'll be here on top. If it goes up we'll all go together'.

Johnstone wrote:

There was nothing more to say, I went over . . . and down into the water. The ship was rising and falling to a slight swell . . . the cable tightening and slacking to my hand. I could see the mine rising and falling away from me. I slid down, passing the mine and getting under it. The water was very clear, and I could see above me the raw unpainted bottom of the *Claymore*. The anchor cable slanting downward, and the mine, its detonating horns like tiny fingers on a huge podgy hand. I could hear the air pump being worked, the voices of my friends on deck.

It was awkward working under the mine. I could see the U-shaped part Captain Williams had mentioned. I managed to shackle it [the wire] to the mine.

But as Johnstone worked under the mine his shot line—his guiding line to the surface—naturally went directly above him. Johnstone didn't realise, but the men on the surface could see what was happening. His shot line was winding itself between the horns of the mine. Williams, who was watching from the whaleboat wrote: 'Johnstone began jerking the shot rope and calling through the phone ... "Slack the shot rope ... slack the shot rope" ... to be told "stop jerking it, it's between two of the horns".'

Johnstone stopped jerking the shot rope. Underwater he had managed to shackle the cable from the minesweeper to the mine. But as he went to move clear the minesweeper moved, the cable tightened and the mine came directly at him.

'I felt myself going down', Johnstone wrote, 'and grabbed at what was nearest, to find myself soaring up. I was almost on the mine, gripping the detonating horns'.

As he lay on the mine, gripping its horns, the cable to the *Humphrey* continued to tighten, pulling the mine up under the *Claymore*.

'I felt, rather than saw the ship's stem close to my head and then my back weights struck'.

The first mine the crew had encountered, the one they had discovered when they first tested the observation chamber three days earlier, now had Johnstone, in his hard-hat diving suit, sandwiched underwater between it and the hull of the *Claymore*.

He waited tense seconds. The *Humphrey* moved and the cable to the mine slackened. The mine dropped, releasing Johnstone from where he'd been trapped, then it suddenly shot to the surface in the direction of the whaleboat. Arthur Bryant, who was in the whaleboat, recalled what happened next.

The mine plunged to the surface ... it really leapt out of the water about three feet. I was standing quite close to it and for a split ... I've never admitted this to anyone before ... but for a split second I turned away from Captain Williams, lost my breakfast and immediately turned back, wrapped my arms and one leg around the mine and was able to hold it without allowing it to rub the ship's side or bump the boat we were in. Whether I was there a minute or an hour I would have no idea.

The mine was held clear and Johnstone hauled back aboard the whaleboat. As he clambered in he was told that the cable he had worked so hard to shackle to the mine had snapped and the mine was still around the *Claymore*'s anchor. The entry in the *Claymore*'s logbook describes what happened next:

Hove mooring up again to bring mine in sight, going slow astern meantime. Its hawsers took the strain and straightened out. Mine again breached the surface about fifty feet from the *Claymore* stern. Engine kept at slow astern. Ship dragging anchor and mine with her.

With all the activity the mine had moved along the anchor line. Now when the *Claymore* moved astern the mine would not come up underneath it, but about 50 feet away. Williams, Johnstone and Arthur Bryant got into the whaleboat and went to the *Humphrey* to discuss what should be tried next.

Williams suggested that now the mine was 50 feet clear of the *Claymore* they could take a cable from the *Humphrey* and simply motor the whaleboat around the mine, looping the cable around it. This was agreed. Williams, Johnstone and Arthur Bryant again got into the whaleboat. Williams wrote:

After getting the wire all ready Arthur Bryant, Johnstone and I towed it back, but just as we were passing between the stern of the *Claymore* and the mine, the [mine] sweeper, for some inconceivable reason, held on and dragged us sideways onto it.

Arthur and I threw the wire off our boat and pushed the mine off her side with our hands, an easy enough thing, the wire being clear, when in the middle of it all, Johnstone got his feet in the manila line going out with the wire, fell half over the side and was hanging with his head in the water.

A complete 'hurrah's nest' if ever you saw one. However in a minute we were clear and fished Johnstone up none the worse, but another failure.

I went back to the sweeper and after an exchange of compliments on his dragging us onto the damned mine, it was decided he [Lieutenant Nielson] should stream his paravane.

A paravane can be likened to an underwater kite. In fact many seamen refer to them as kites. A torpedo-shaped object with fins, it is attached by a long line to the minesweeper. When the minesweeper moves at speed the paravane—underwater—streams out to the side of the ship, pulling the line tight. It was Nielson's plan to rig a paravane out to the side of the *Humphrey* and, passing the *Claymore* at speed, run the paravane between the *Claymore* and the mine. It would not be an easy task. For the paravane to work it would have to be streamed out almost a mile. From this distance, and at speed, Nielson would have to guide the paravane through a gap of about 50 feet. Too close and the paravane would cut the *Claymore*'s anchor line as well and all the work would go for naught. Too far away and he would simply miss. There were two other possibilities. The paravane could hit the *Claymore*, almost certainly driving a hole into its rusting hull. Or, very unlikely, it could hit the mine and detonate it.

The plan was agreed upon and Williams, Johnstone and Bryant returned to the *Claymore* in the whaleboat. As they had done all day, the majority of the *Claymore* crew stayed on the minesweeper for safety. The logbook reads: 'Sweeper rigged float and kite gear. Stood off about one mile and steamed in . . . float missed *Claymore* hull by about one foot and cut mooring of mine'. Arthur Bryant described it to me as 'a fairly neat piece of work'.

Finally the mine mooring line had been cut. The *Claymore* released its anchor line and this stayed afloat, trapped with the mine now bobbing in the water. It was Williams' plan to net the mine, tow it ashore, and salvage his precious anchor and line. But Williams, like Johnstone, was not having a good day. Before leaving the *Humphrey* he had explained his intentions to the crew, but for some reason those instructions were ignored.

Before the majority of the *Claymore* crew had been put aboard the *Humphrey* earlier that day, Johnstone had given one of them his 16 mm movie camera. Now someone filmed the *Claymore* crew members and New Zealand naval ratings. The black and white film that survives shows the men smiling and posing with their guns, it shows the mine bobbing in the water, it shows the men firing at the mine with the 5.9 inch navy gun, its shows spurts of water near the mine as the shells and bullets narrowly miss it, it shows men taking pot shots with a rifle and finally it shows a huge camera-shaking eruption as the mine explodes in a massive volcano of water.

The film, however, doesn't show what was happening on the *Claymore* standing off about a mile away. For Williams and Johnstone it must have been a frustrating sight. They'd risked their lives repeatedly to keep the mine and their anchor line afloat. If they'd wanted to simply cut it free and sink it they could have done that the first day. Now they had to stand off in the *Claymore* and watch their own crew and the New Zealand Navy ignore Williams' instructions and for some inexplicable reason, happily sink it. This would have been made more frustrating by the fact that Williams had no way of communicating with the *Humphrey* to tell them to stop. He had repeatedly asked the Navy for the use of a radio aboard the *Claymore* and the Navy had repeatedly refused to let him have one.

Williams was a man of many fine attributes, but in all my interviews and research, I was never to find evidence that forgiveness was one of them. My imagination is not broad enough to speculate at what he might have said when the *Claymore* finally came back alongside the *Humphrey*. The matter only receives a brief comment in the logbook: '*Claymore* full astern and stood away while Sweeper's gun fired on mine and sank it. Protested against this before happening advising Commander of Sweeper that we would net mine and tow it away but was not heeded'.

For John Johnstone, wrestling with the mine had left him exhausted. 'I just did not feel I wanted to go below again—not for a day or so, anyhow'. The *Claymore* returned to Whangarei. Williams drove to Auckland and purchased another anchor.

*   *   *

Before the *Niagara* had sunk, its last fixed position had been obtained at 3.34 a.m. This placed it in a position with the Moko Hinau Light bearing 94 degrees and the Chicken Island's Light 274 degrees. For the following nine minutes the ship continued on a course true North until 3.43 a.m. when it had hit the mine. At this point the ship sheered to starboard, gradually losing speed. It remained afloat for over two hours and sank at 5.53 a.m. The tide at the time was running south at the rate of one knot.

Bill Reynolds of Whangarei, who had been awakened by his father to go in the family launch to rescue passengers, recalled:

The first boat we picked up—we picked it up because it was the furthest out to sea—contained the Chief Officer, the Fourth Officer, the Bosun, Bosun's Mate, Chief Steward and several seamen.

Now the Chief Officer, his name was Gibson—unfortunately we did not pick up the captain because he transferred to a boat with a wireless set after daylight—however Chief Office Gibson was very good. He helped me quite a lot gathering these people out of the lifeboats. Some of them were quite sick and were suffering with fright and all that sort of thing and I was very busy getting cups of tea and so forth.

I gave him the wheel of the *Menai* to go for the next boat, you see, sometimes they were a mile apart—a mile and a half apart—and I said to him, 'Where do you think she is?' That is, the *Niagara*.

And he took a pin from under the lapel of his jacket, studied the chart for a while and he said, 'I think she's there.' And he pushed the pin through the chart—ordinary Admiralty chart'.

The fact that the *Niagara* had sunk within sight of land, with various islands around from which bearings could be taken, meant the search area would be small. Williams had a square with each side three miles long marked out with float buoys. Nine square miles in which he hoped to find the *Niagara*. A square with each side 5 280 feet long in which to find a ship approximately one tenth that length.

He began searching with a circular sweep. The crew would drop an anchor at a point and steam around it in ever widening circles, waiting for the line to catch on something . . .

* * *

While the *Claymore* was doing this, Naval Messages were being exchanged between Wellington and Auckland. On 4 January, Commander Bingley at Auckland received a message from Wellington saying:

Position of mine given by '*Humphrey*' is well clear of area swept for salvage operations. Captain Williams should be warned that if he leaves the swept area he is running into danger and that future salvage operations will be immediately stopped by order of New Zealand Naval Board. Request you will keep a watch on movements of *Claymore* and report if instructions are not carried out.

At sea, Williams continued sweeping the new area until 7 January when, according to the logbook a Naval patrol boat approached the *Claymore* and:

... shouted to the watch that Commander Bingley of the Naval Depot Auckland wished Captain Williams to telephone him at the latter's earliest convenience. It was explained to the person in charge of the patrol boat that the *Claymore* would not return to port saving through bad weather or lack of water and coal.

Then, later in the day: 'Naval patrol vessel returned with the same message as before. After consideration Master decided to return to Urquharts Bay as it was felt unwise to risk antagonising Naval Authority'.

The *Claymore* returned to Urquharts Bay, from where Williams telephoned the Commander. He was told that work was not to continue until the area he had buoyed was swept. Williams' reply is not recorded anywhere, but at 5 a.m. the next day the *Claymore* put to sea again and continued sweeping. At 12.25 the sweep wire separated. It was hauled in and found to be cut through cleanly. A mine was suspected but not found.

The next few days were spent at anchor in the lee of the Maro Tiri Islands, waiting for the weather to clear. It did on 13 January and sweeping recommenced.

A day later, at 11 a.m., the sweep caught something. It was another mine.

This mine popped up five feet from the moving *Claymore*. The crew watched as it passed slowly down the port side, coming closer to the rusting hull plates.

It touched.

Fifty years later Ray Nelson still recalled with horror the sound of the metal scraping against the hull. 'It made contact with the bow and slid, slid slowly along the side of the ship. You could hear it grating on the plates of the hull. You know, everyone stood there mesmerised, not able to move. Just as well someone did. It was Arthur Bryant.'

With luck the mine might have passed, except the whaleboat was tied aft on the port side and the mine was heading straight for it. Arthur Bryant was first to see the situation. He ran along the deck, leapt into the whaleboat, undid its mooring rope and pushed it away from the *Claymore* with all his strength. Within seconds he watched the mine pass through the gap he had created.

The mine was tied off to a buoy and the *Claymore*, having now gained the title of 'The Ship That No Mine Can Sink', returned to Urquharts Bay where, from the Manaia Gardens Guest House, Williams could use the telephone. This time he rang the Naval Depot in Wellington and was told that the *Muritai*, commanded by Commander Holden, Director of Sweeping, would come to Urquharts Bay the next morning.

Williams and Johnstone went aboard the *Muritai* when it arrived and proceeded to the buoyed area. While sweeping the mine they had buoyed the day before, a second mine was also found. The first was exploded with a one-inch shell. The second was sunk by gunfire. At this time Williams decided to return to Whangarei for coal and water. The logbook of 16 January reports:

Mr Johnstone reported that M. Paulson and J. Thompson expressed their intention to desert the ship at the first opportunity and further that they were making every effort to sow dissention amongst the crew in the hope of holding up the ship and bringing the venture to a close thereby.

It was five weeks since the *Claymore* had steamed away from the wharf in Auckland. The men were tired and morale was low. There had been no sign of the *Niagara*. And when the weather had allowed them to search, all they had found were mines that on two occasions had nearly killed them. Williams' single-mindedness about the salvage had got them this far. In their later accounts, Johnstone and Williams described the time as a low point in the salvage.

But it was also a turning point.

For on 16 January, while Williams was writing about the troubles of the crew in the *Claymore*'s logbook, another man was writing in his personal diary. His entry for 16 January consisted of only two words: 'Joined *Claymore*'.

FOUR

16 January – 3 February 1941

A Finer Lot of Chaps I Have Never Met

In my travels and interviews I encountered men who spoke highly of Captain Williams, but who were reluctant to say much about John Johnstone. I encountered men who praised Johnstone, but were reluctant to talk about Williams. I soon got in the habit of unofficially labelling my interviewee as either a 'Johnstone man' or a 'Williams man'. But there was one thing on which 'Williams men' and 'Johnstone men' universally agreed. They all had the highest regard for Captain James Herd.

'When Captain Herd joined the *Claymore* we became a team', Ray Nelson told me.

Due to business commitments, James Herd was not able to join the crew until the middle of January. From his home in Queensland, he flew to Sydney, then sailed to New Zealand where he joined the *Claymore*.

Herd kept a diary during the entire year he was with the *Claymore*, but in it he wrote only the briefest comments. In fact his diary reads very much like the ship's logbook, recording weather details, the number of times the chamber was lowered, problems with the mooring buoys and the general business of the ship. But James Herd also wrote letters home to his wife. And in these he expressed not only his feelings, but a personal account of what was happening aboard the *Claymore*.

Over 50 years later James Herd's daughter lent me these personal letters, and in the frail yellow pages that cracked and split as I unfolded them I found an independent, first-hand account of the salvage. Not written as a newspaper account. Nor written with hindsight to glorify or justify one's actions. But simple, honest writing from a man to his wife that began to tell me the story that was behind the public account. And the men of the *Claymore* began to take on a life and reality that I couldn't feel through their official correspondence and records.

On 16 January 1941, the same day that he wrote in his diary that he had 'Joined *Claymore*', Captain James Herd also wrote to his wife. In part the letter read:

The job [*Niagara*] is not found yet but the area is being well swept by another vessel fitted for sweeping. You will have to consider this yourself as censorship might not let me fully describe this job. We shall be out for perhaps two weeks but I shall write as often as possible, a launch comes in at least once a week and will post and collect letters.

I saw all the gear today, it is very efficient. There are good divers, shipwrights, blacksmiths, engineers, etc on board and they look a likely looking lot of chaps to work with.

I am now looking forward to starting work and have a hunch that it is going to be a most fascinating and interesting job. John Johnstone the Chief Diver . . . has been down over 400 feet in the chamber and states that everything worked very efficiently. I had a look inside today, it is fitted with all sorts of useful gadgets, even a clock to tell the time by.

In Captain James Herd, Williams found the perfect second-in-command. Herd would talk to the men and listen to them. He would patiently explain things. Later on he arranged evening classes aboard the *Claymore* to teach the younger sailors the arts of traditional mariners—how to read charts, plot courses, take sextant bearings and so on. When the Johnstone brothers were exhausted from the stress of their diving, when Captain Williams would confine himself in his cabin for hours to work at problems, or later because of illness, Herd looked after the men.

*　　*　　*

In the seven months since the *Niagara* had sunk, the Battle of Britain had been fought in the skies over the English Channel. The Royal Air Force had stopped the Luftwaffe and proved that the British Isles would not be overrun as easily as the rest of Western Europe.

Smarting from the fact that Germans were not marching through London, Hitler's tactic now was to try to starve the British into submission. His Directive Number 23 was 'to concentrate every means of waging war by sea and air on enemy supplies'. At the beginning of 1941 the Germans were sinking allied merchant ships at a rate of over two a day—faster than they could be built. Forty-eight million Britons had their food severely rationed, while supplies of food from Commonwealth countries struggled to reach the 'mother country'.

When war had been declared in September 1939, the Australian Prime Minister, Robert Menzies, declared his support for Great Britain pointing out that Australians were 'a British people . . . fitted to face the crisis with cheerful fortitude and confidence'.

At the time the majority of Australians were indeed a 'British people'. But that didn't necessarily mean that Australia should sacrifice everything to help Great Britain. There was also a public feeling that perhaps Australia had no business sending troops to Europe to fight. The expansionist plans of the Japanese in the Pacific were well known. Should not Australian soldiers be staying home to be prepared to defend their own soil?

For Prime Minister Menzies there was no question. Australia would support Britain. But he was also conscious of the fact that his attitude did not make him popular with a large section of the electorate.

* * *

In Whangarei, Williams prepared to continue his search for the *Niagara*. But first he spoke to the crew members who had 'expressed their intention to desert the ship'. Paulson and Thompson gave as their reasons for sowing dissension the fact that they had not been told, before leaving Australia, that the work would include sweeping mines. They also stated the crew were not insured for 'War Risk'. Paulson additionally stated that he considered the *Claymore* undermanned and unsafe.

Williams paid their fares back to Australia.

On 17 January the *Claymore* put to sea again to continue the search. On this trip the *Claymore* spent a week over the search area which was progressively swept with trawling wires, but there was no sign of the *Niagara*.

The week's search was uneventful, except for one incident in which Herd was to prove his usefulness on his first trip out. On the night of 22 January, when the sea was rough, Arthur Bryant and John Johnstone noticed that the whaleboat being towed by the *Claymore* was filling with water. At Johnstone's suggestion they got in and started baling it out. The *Claymore* rose and fell. In a see-saw action at the other end of the rope, so did the whaleboat. Herd walked aft and saw the pair rising and falling, first on the crest of a wave, then out of view. He realised the danger of the situation and yelled to them to get out of the boat.

Arthur Bryant was no seaman and perhaps could be excused for not understanding the danger. Johnstone, with his knowledge of ships, should have known better. But the pair continued baling out the whaleboat.

Herd yelled at them again, and again they ignored him. The third time he swore at them in such a manner that, startled, they stopped what they were doing and began to climb back aboard the *Claymore*. As they did so the ship rose and came down directly on top of the whaleboat, smashing it to pieces. It sank from view. The pair had escaped death by a matter of seconds.

A day later the *Claymore* returned to Whangarei.

While the *Claymore* had been riding out the storm and destroying its whaleboat, Commander Bingley of the Naval Base at Auckland, had sent a message to the New Zealand Naval Headquarters in Wellington:

Niagara has not – repeat not – been located contrary to report given me by Williams.

Williams assured me again he would not – repeat not – proceed outside swept area.

Consider he is not – repeat not – to be trusted to adhere to this.

. . . suggest work be stopped at present.

This time the Navy were going to take no chances and the Chief of Naval Staff, aware of the political push behind Williams, wrote to the New Zealand Minister of Defence on 24 January, informing him:

> ... From the position in which the obstruction was encountered and the mines swept it became evident that the position of the *Niagara* had not been established. This was contrary to the report which Captain Williams had made to the Naval Officer in Charge, Auckland, and it also showed that Captain Williams had proceeded outside the swept area in spite of assurances he had given to the Naval Officer in Charge that he would not do so.
>
> As it is apparent that Captain Williams is not entirely to be relied upon, and in view of the danger to the *Claymore*, I have given directions that further operations are to be stopped until further clearance has been carried out.
>
> Arrangements for such clearance will be made as soon as practicable.

In Whangarei, Williams was instructed to wait before taking the *Claymore* to sea again. Impatient to continue, and ignoring the fact that he was searching for the *Niagara* outside of the designated search area, in an area still not cleared of mines, he wrote to the Governor of the Commonwealth Bank in Australia:

> I have just received a telephone message from the Commander of the Naval Depot in Auckland to the effect that the Naval Board forbid the carrying out of further sweeping operations until the area has been cleared of mines. In answer to my enquiry as to when this was likely to be I received the usual reply, that it was impossible to say. Personally I find it most difficult to see why, if it has been good enough for us to work until now there should be any alteration at this juncture.
>
> Will you please take the matter up with the authorities and ask them to do whatever they consider necessary without any further delay so that we may get on with the work without interruption.

The bank, however, chose not to 'take the matter up' with the authorities. The secretary of the bank wrote a note in the margin of Williams, letter saying: 'I do not think Commonwealth authorities would agree to approach the New Zealand Government in a matter which is entirely within the discretion of the latter'.

* * *

In Whangarei, Williams would simply have to wait for the New Zealand Navy to clear the area where he now wanted to search.

After his first week at sea on the job, James Herd wrote to his wife.

. . . After eleven years ashore with the sweetest little girl I ever knew, sea going was at first a bit strange but it's remarkable how soon it all comes back to one, the seamanship part of the job is simple enough but it took a day or so to refresh my memory and get the hang of the navigational side of it. I had not had a sextant in my hand since I left the sea, far less using one, but a couple of days practice and all my troubles were overcome.

Our Chief Diver has a movie camera and he is continually taking shots, someday I may have the opportunity of having the films shown to you, they will be very interesting and will make a good picture. So far the job has not been very interesting but it will be as time goes on.

There are fifteen of us working on this job and a finer lot of chaps I have never met, not one snag among them. The wag of the ship is Danny Scott our blacksmith, a Belfast man who has been all over the place mostly, through the oil fields of America, he was at one time a steeplejack in New York. Last night he came to my cabin with a pile of photographs taken of himself climbing steeples and high buildings at New York, also some photographs taken on various oilfields. He kept me in roars of laughter spinning yarns about various men with whom he has worked. Danny came across from Melbourne with John Williams. At meal time he has everyone in fits—I never met a better entertainer than Dan Scott.

While the *Claymore* waited to return to the search area another crew member joined. I had read about Leslie Mischewski in contemporary accounts of the *Niagara* salvage. He had joined the *Claymore* as 'cook's assistant' but had so impressed Williams with his attitude and hard work, he had been promoted to 'deck hand'. At sixteen years of age he was the youngest of the New Zealanders that Williams would hire. Because of his age I thought he might be still alive. This turned out to be so, as Les Mischewski wrote to me in response to the press releases I put in Whangarei papers: 'As the youngest crew member on board *Claymore* at the time I may well be one of only a few surviving. I am 67 years old now and have an unclouded memory of the entire operation.'

When I met and interviewed Les Mischewski he explained how he came to join the *Claymore*:

I was working at the Regent Theatre and I went down to get a haircut on Cameron Street and the hairdresser, McKinnon, asked me if I wanted a job on the ship. He had just finished cutting the captain's [Williams] hair, and I said yeah. So he said 'go down to Kiorera' [Wharf]. It was an old metal road at the time and I was on the pushbike. The *Claymore* was tied up there. So I saw the captain, he put me on to Stan Mitchell, the steward and I got the job.

* * *

After waiting five days in Whangarei, during which time Mischewski joined the crew, Williams received a message that the New Zealand Navy were sending a minesweeper to clear the area he now wanted to search. The *Claymore* steamed down Whangarei Harbour and anchored at Urquharts Bay, where Williams went aboard RNZN Minesweeper *Muritai* and met with Commander Holden. Holden explained he would need two days to sweep the area that Williams wanted to search. Williams waited at Urquharts Bay. The *Muritai* recovered one mine and on 31 January 1941 the *Claymore* then 'hove up and proceeded to sea'.

Williams later wrote that, arriving at what he thought was the search area, he was unable to see any of the marker buoys. Believing he was in the search area the sweep was 'streamed' and the *Claymore* steamed north. The sweep itself at this point was a 'square sweep'. Two trawl wires were streamed from the rear of the *Claymore*. At the end of each was an 'otter' board. Like the paravane, the boards worked on the 'kite' principal and, in this case, pulled the two trawl wires in opposite directions. But between the two trawl wires was a third wire. This third wire, the sweep wire, was pulled tight and as the *Claymore* moved forward it would scrape the seabed. The sweep wire was 600 feet long. As the *Claymore* steamed up and down the search area it swept a path 600 feet wide. Today, salvage crews sometimes refer to this process as 'mowing the lawn'.

The *Claymore* was not in the designated search area for as it steamed north, dragging its trawl wire, it actually caught and fouled the marker buoy at the south-west corner of the search area. The salvage ship was well to the south of where it was supposed to be. The buoy was fouled at 7.10 a.m. The sweep wire pulled the drum marker buoy underwater, probably to a depth of around 200 feet where it had immediately been crushed by the water pressure. The crew were left to wrestle with a tangled mess of wires which took them about two hours to sort out. Because the wires were hanging over the stern, the engine could not be started for fear of fouling the propeller. The *Claymore* drifted slowly to the west, away from the search area, and again into an area which had not yet been swept of mines.

Williams and James Herd were helping untangle the wires as the *Claymore* continued to drift. Williams left instructions with Billy Green, who was at the wheel, that when he heard the engine start he was to head east, back to the search area. Finally the wires were untangled and the engine started. Williams noticed the *Claymore* was heading north.

He wrote that he thought, 'oh hell, we don't know where we are anyway', went to the bridge and instructed Billy Green to steer east, then went to the galley to get a cup of tea. He had taken a sip when the trawl wire winch screamed a sharp metallic scream and the wires became as tight and as straight as steel rods.

Something had been hooked. Something large.

A marker buoy was put over to indicate the spot and the trawl and sweep wires hauled in.

From the tender *Betsy*, the diesel-engined tender, James Herd took soundings around the area. This was done with a sounding weight—a lead weight attached to a line. A hollow in the weight contained tallow, so that when it hit the bottom, particles of whatever was there would stick to it. The weight was repeatedly lowered to 68 fathoms (408 feet). Each time it returned to the surface the tallow contained particles of sand. Then the weight stopped at 58 fathoms. Sixty feet short of the seabed. (The *Niagara* was 66 feet across at its widest point.) The lead weight was brought aboard *Betsy*. Now stuck to the tallow were small flakes of paint. Three distinct colours could be identified. Red, grey and a pale brownish yellow.

The *Niagara* had been painted first with a red metal primer. For many years it had been painted grey, but at the outbreak of war the owners felt the grey made it look too much like a warship and had it repainted. When it sank the hull had been painted buff—or pale brownish yellow.

The paint flakes, still stuck in the tallow, were carefully taken aboard the *Claymore* and shown to Williams. He in turn showed them to Ray Nelson, who identified the colour as being identical to that of the ship he had been serving on when it had sunk. Although it still had to be positively confirmed, Williams felt he had found his ship and was confident enough to write in the logbook: 'Vessel considered found at last'.

Half a century later, to the day, on 31 January 1991, 'the wag of the ship', Danny Scott, died in a nursing home at the age of 93. The chain of events that followed led me to find the story of the recovery of the gold from the *Niagara*.

*   *   *

Williams now had to establish how the ship lay on the seabed. A day was spent, without success, lowering the sounding weight to try and determine this. It was decided to send John Johnstone down in the chamber to see if he could visually confirm they had the right ship.

The next day was fine, clear and calm. Williams attempted to bring the *Claymore* over the wreck, dragging the bow anchor so as to 'hook' it. This at first proved difficult and it was not until 4 p.m. that the observation chamber could be lowered.

'Take no chances, Johnstone,' Williams had said to him. 'All I want is for you to confirm that it's her'.

Johnstone wrote:

I was soon swinging out from the ship and being lowered, already feeling myself being lifted and dropped as the ship rolled. Down I went, the water coming up past my windows. The bell was spinning around, a movement caused by the spiral lay of the wire rope, and this on top of the up and down movement soon had me feeling horribly seasick.

The chamber reached the bottom and settled softly in the mud before it began to be pulled sideways.

'Not much I can do about that', Williams said to Johnstone. 'The tide has us'.

'Take me up ten or fifteen feet', Johnstone said back.

As Williams was unable to have the *Claymore* held in position because of the tides, the chamber was lifted about ten feet above the seabed and drifted along with Johnstone looking out the portholes. He could see objects on the seabed as they glided by beneath him: 'Many objects too. They were shiny tins, then what I took to be a suitcase and boxes. The most promising trip yet . . . '

There was a crash. The light in the chamber went out and Johnstone was thrown off his feet. Through the telephone he called urgently to the surface to take him up as he struggled to regain his feet in the narrow confines of the chamber. The chamber started to rise and Johnstone looked out the portholes. He could faintly make out lifeboat davits. As he steadied himself the chamber continued to rise and the ship disappeared from view. The chief diver's introduction to the RMS *Niagara* had been brief.

Once on the surface, Johnstone was able to give a full report of what he had seen. Although he was unable to tell on which side the ship lay, or in which direction, he was able to confirm it was the *Niagara*.

The next day Williams steamed the *Claymore* around in circles, again dragging his bow anchor to hook the wreck. But the morning's activities were not successful. Firstly the bow anchor and 40 fathoms of holding wire were lost. Then the rope attached to a second anchor fouled the propeller and the *Claymore* drifted helplessly for four hours before John Johnstone, in his hard-hat diving dress, went over the side and cleared it. In the afternoon the *Claymore* was back in position and the observation chamber made ready.

Johnstone was lowered again. By this time the chamber had been down to 400 feet four times. It had withstood the pressure of the depth without problem. But other difficulties had been discovered.

Firstly, lowering it underwater was proving difficult. In fact when the chamber was half-submerged, it was extremely awkward to handle. Williams explained this in a letter to the chamber's designer, David Isaacs:

> ... makes the operation of putting it over the side one of some danger. The worst time appears to be when it is semi-buoyant and the lurch of the ship away from it gives it an upward momentum, so much so indeed, that it jumps three feet out of the water and, then when the ship comes back the other way, crashes down on the gear in a somewhat alarming fashion.

When the chamber was half-submerged, the half out of the water still 'weighed' a ton or more while the half under the water, before the diver had filled the ballast tanks with sea water, 'weighed' around 100–200 pounds.

In fact John Johnstone found the whole experience so violent he was constantly vomiting. After his first trips in the chamber he adopted the habit of wearing gum boots, because he found that once it was submerged he would then be forced to work underwater for hours with no choice but to stand in his own vomit.

Also, in an attempt to reduce the violent bucking as it was lowered underwater, Johnstone put a length of heavy steel chain in the bottom of the chamber. When he learnt of this David Isaacs wrote to Williams expressing concern:

> ... the present operations ... render such ballast chains inadvisable. The reason for this inadvisability is that the chamber was originally designed to come to the surface if fouled (a) by blowing air into the buoyancy chamber or (b) by dropping off one or two cast iron weights or (c) by using both air and dropping off weights.
>
> The total amount of lift or buoyancy available to the diver, even under condition (c) where both air and dropping of cast iron weights are adopted to bring the chamber towards the surface, is not great; where only (a) or (b) is used the lift is quite small. Therefore the carrying of ballast chains may seriously upset the emergency operation of the chamber.

On 3 February, the logbook of the *Claymore* records that the wreck was hooked at 3.05 p.m. and the chamber 'put over'. A choppy sea was running and the chamber was jerking up and down violently.

But this time it was a bulls-eye. Johnstone's plan was to try and land the chamber on the *Niagara* and have the holding wire slacked off. In this way the *Claymore* could rise and fall as it liked, while he could sit stationary on the wreck. This would allow him to observe and sketch features of the *Niagara* to discover how it lay on the seabed.

He gave instructions over the telephone to the crew handling the chamber above. He was moved, first this way, then that . . . then lowered and positioned successfully on the wreck. He called for the wire to be slacked off, then looked out at the scene that lay before him. This was Johnstone's first clear look at the *Niagara* and he wrote:

I could see more now. The *Niagara* was almost on her side. One funnel had fallen and hung on the ship's side. The other stood up solidly. I could see the promenade deck with its white painted handrails, boat davits with rope falls still dangling as they had been left when the boats were lowered. I could see doorways and long rows of portholes, everything seemed frozen in this underwater grave. I was sketching as I looked, making careful diagrams . . .

On the surface the anchor line holding the *Claymore* snapped. The salvage ship started to swing away with the wind. The wire holding the chamber suddenly jerked tight.

Johnstone had no time to think or react. The chamber was suddenly jerked from where it had been sitting upright on the *Niagara*. It was dragged sideways, Johnstone being bounced around inside. It narrowly missed the lifeboat davits he'd just been sketching, then slid down the side of the wreck. It landed upside down in the soft seabed, Johnstone crashing into the steel lid. He had a split-second to recover, to try and understand what was going on, before the chamber began bouncing and being dragged along the seabed.

Above, Williams and the crew could not know what was happening to Johnstone in the chamber. The obvious thought was to quickly wind in the wire and bring him to the surface. But the *Claymore* kept drifting before the wind. Its decrepit boilers didn't have enough steam up to both propel the ship and work the winch. Williams ordered the winch to wind up the chamber. *Betsy*, was brought around and her bow put against the side of the *Claymore*.

While the crew tried to bring the chamber on board, the small tender strained to try and hold the *Claymore* from drifting further.

At 5.20 p.m., two hours and fifteen minutes after he was lowered over the side, the logbook recorded that the diver was brought safely on board.

Johnstone was lifted bodily out of the chamber by members of the crew, who carried him to his bunk, towelled the blood off him and gave him a cigarette.

He records that he said, 'Don't ever do that again'.

After that dive another item joined the gumboots as part of his diving 'uniform'. He bought a safety helmet of the style worn by racing cyclists to protect his head from being battered against the sides of the chamber.

FIVE

4 February – 7 March 1941

The Job Would Not Be Very Complicated

Today, using satellite navigation linked to an onboard computer controlling a multi-propulsion system, a well-equipped salvage vessel can hold its position—even in a gale—to within three feet in any direction. The computer reads the information from satellites in space. Then it adjusts the speed of the revolutions of the propellers positioned around the ship. And the ship stays exactly where the captain wants it.

In 1941 Williams had no such luxuries. Satellite navigation was unknown to the world and to the *Claymore*, which had been built in Scotland and launched a year before the Wright brothers made the first powered flight. Nor would computers have had a place on a ship without electricity and whose only means of light was kerosene lamps. Nor did the *Claymore* have a multi-propulsion system—it had one propeller at the stern and that had a blade missing. So even when under steam the engine could not be run fast for fear that the unbalanced propeller would vibrate violently and damage the shaft.

Not, of course, that the engine was in much danger of forcing the broken propeller to turn too quickly. Manufactured by Muir and Houston in Scotland, the triple-expansion steam-driven engine was rated to 55 horsepower and also dated from 1902, six years before Henry Ford manufactured the first T-model.

But in this rusting, leaking, underpowered ship Williams had to devise a method of holding position over the wreck of the *Niagara* with such accuracy that, even when waves and swell were rocking the *Claymore*, even when tides and currents were trying to carry it up or down the Hauraki Gulf, even when winds were buffeting it, that a steel chamber could be lowered 400 feet to within a few inches of a position below.

Accuracy in lowering the chamber was one problem. Getting it in and out of the water had proven another. There were still others.

One was the rolling of the *Claymore* on the swell or the waves, and the strain this put on the cable, winches and lifting gear. This problem can best be understood if the reader considers a heavy sinker, underwater, held via fishing line to a flexible fishing rod. If the sinker is sitting on the seabed and the line is slack, then the fishing rod can be raised and lowered slightly without feeling the weight of the sinker. If, however, the sinker is suspended in the water, not touching the seabed, and the rod is raised and lowered, the weight of the sinker will tug at the rod as it is lifted, then as the rod is lowered the line will go momentarily slack—underwater gravity acts in slow motion—before the weight of the sinker jerks on the line.

The *Claymore* would roll on the surface. Protruding from its starboard side was a short 'fishing rod'. And suspended from that rod, on 400 feet of wire, was a man inside a steel chamber. Williams later wrote:

In my innocence I thought that considering its [the chamber's] weight, as the *Claymore* rolled to it, so it would go down and come up as she rose and rolled the other way. Nothing of the kind however. As the ship rolled to the bell, sure it went down, but when she rose the bell still wanted to go down. The bell wire now a harp string—threatening to tear the winch from the deck and taking two men to hold it around the [winch] drum end, and this repeated at every roll. I expected at any minute to see the *Claymore*'s mast go with a jerk, or the shaft of the winch break or the bell wire part and disaster overwhelm us. Jim Herd and I sat down to think about it all.

Another problem was that the chamber would turn in a corkscrew manner as it descended. It would spin in a clockwise direction, 'winding up' the wire on which it was suspended. It would unwind itself as it ascended and by the time it reached the surface would be almost back to its original position. But on the way down and up it would spin so much that either John or Bill Johnstone would become ill, while the spinning made observation out of the small portholes extremely difficult.

These problems with the observation chamber had not been anticipated by Williams and they now joined a growing list of concerns he must have felt early in February 1941. For not only was he having difficulty handling the observation chamber, the *Niagara*, now that it had been found, was not lying in the position he had expected.

Six months earlier, during his trip to New Zealand to study the feasibility of recovering the gold, he had found an object rising approximately 120 feet from the bottom. Williams was confident it was the *Niagara*. He had also been confident the ship, which was only 66 feet wide but over 120 feet high, was therefore sitting upright. In his initial report to the bank he had written:

If the possibility of cutting through the ship from above is considered, it should be noted that 'A' deck is of .20 inch plate, 'B' deck of .24 inch plate and 'C' deck of .52 inch plate whilst it is also probable though not certain that a doubling plate has been fitted to the top of the bullion room.

'A' deck is clear of obstruction . . . on both 'B' and 'C' decks above the room are lavatories and bathrooms of which the floors are cemented and tiled.

Williams had been confident that he could blast his way through the three decks, then into the top of the bullion room. But his 'object rising 120 feet from the seabed' proved to be natural formation. Now, with the *Niagara* found lying on its side, it was a different matter. And, as yet, it was not established on which side it lay. In his initial report he had noted:

If it chances however, that the *Niagara* has come to rest on the port side at an angle of 90 degrees with the vertical, then the job would not be very complicated. The Chief Steward's room is situated on the vessel's side, abreast of the strong room; an alleyway of some four feet in width running between the two.

That is, if the ship lay with its starboard side up, Williams would need only to blast a way through the outer hull, the steward's room then cross an open hallway to reach the bullion room door.

'If on the other hand she lies on her starboard side, considerable difficulty may be anticipated.'

An understatement to say the least. For if the *Niagara* lay with its starboard side down, the bullion room would be buried under the bulk of the ship and blasting a way to it would be difficult to the point of impossibility.

Williams had an even chance between having a task which would 'not be very complicated', and a task where 'considerable difficulty may be anticipated'. But due to the problems he still had to overcome with the chamber and methods of mooring the *Claymore* above the wreck, he would have to wait almost two months before he knew on which side the *Niagara* lay.

* * *

The second syndicate formed to salvage the gold bullion aboard the *Niagara* had it origins in the 1920s with an eccentric Melbourne inventor—one Ernest Clifford. Clifford invented what he described as an 'anti-paralysis diving suit'. As the name implies the suit was supposed to allow a diver to work underwater without suffering the paralysing effects of the bends.

Clifford claimed his 'anti-paralysis diving suit' would allow a diver to work deeper for longer and ascend with virtually no decompression period. His suit was supposed to do this by protecting the diver from the water pressure. In a sense, what he tried to invent was halfway between an regular hard-hat diving suit and an observation chamber. He thought that if his diving suit could somehow protect the head and the chest of the diver from the water pressure, then the effects of that pressure would be reduced. He was not the first to contemplate this idea. Even Leonardo da Vinci had drawn divers with their own air supply and an apparatus like a barrel around their chest to stop the water pressure compressing their lungs.

Clifford patented a number of designs for his diving suit between 1926 and 1933. Each used different methods of relieving pressure on the diver's chest, but generally the idea was to have a diving suit with an inner and outer lining. As the diver went deeper he could fill the air space between the inner and outer lining with compressed air. This compressed air would make the suit rigid, relieving the pressure on the diver's chest.

The idea didn't work. You can't protect half the body from pressure any more than you can send a man into space in half a sealed space capsule.

But in the 1920s and '30s knowledge of diving was still in its infancy and, on paper, Clifford's idea seemed to have enough merit for many people to take it seriously. Clifford wanted a diver to test his suit and as he lived in Melbourne he approached John Johnstone. Johnstone wisely said the suit wouldn't work. He felt so strongly that he began telling others in the diving community it wouldn't work. He only stopped when Clifford threatened him with legal action.

Another diver, John Le Noury, a longtime friend of Johnstone's, believed the idea could work and agreed to test it. This he did in deep water outside Port Phillip Heads, Melbourne, in 1931. Returning to the surface Le Noury felt the paralysis engulf his body and knew the suit had failed. He took three months to die a painful death.

Somewhere around this time Clifford moved from Melbourne to Sydney. With a solicitor, Henry Whatmore, he set up a company called The Austral Submarine Inventions Limited. A number of the 'anti-paralysis diving suits' were manufactured, agents appointed and attempts made to sell them to the pearl-diving industry in Western Australia. These attempts seem to have failed. Clifford meanwhile turned his attention to other inventions.

Feeling his talents were overlooked in Australia he tried to ingratiate himself to the Japanese by offering them his ideas free of charge. His ideas included an artificial wool substitute, a torpedo that tracked a ship by sound—following the noise of the ship's propeller—and oil derived from soya beans. Ideas ahead of their time perhaps, but none of them developed to fruition by Clifford.

Later, after Japan entered the war, Australian Military Intelligence started investigating Clifford's allegiance but discovered the Japanese took him no more seriously than did Australia. When they tracked him down they found him under psychiatric care, decided he was basically a harmless nut and forgot about him.

Clifford's anti paralysis diving suit would probably have passed into obscurity had the *Niagara* not sunk. But Henry Whatmore, now owned four anti-paralysis suits which had been manufactured, along with the rights to manufacture more.

Immediately after the *Niagara* had sunk, it will be recalled, the British Admiralty suggested that naval authorities in Australia investigate the possibility of salvage. The Naval Board in Melbourne then sent its telegram to the District Naval Offices around the country saying: '*Niagara* sunk in 60 fathoms. Request information whether there is diving equipment suitable for working at this depth available in Australia'.

Whatmore was known to the Navy because he and Clifford had previously tried to interest them in buying suits for Navy divers. Now the Navy, under circumstances that were later disputed, approached Whatmore asking if his suit would work at 60 fathoms. Whatmore had said it would. The Navy did not pursue the enquiry and later, when the contract to salvage the *Niagara*'s gold was awarded to John Williams, Henry Whatmore, along with a William Thomson and another solicitor, A. W. Uther, began making plans to salvage the gold for themselves.

Thomson tested the anti-paralysis suit, diving in Sydney Harbour around Blue's Point. Believing it would work, he then met with Uther and Whatmore and the three formed an agreement. The role of the two solicitors would be largely that of finding investors in the project. The actual salvaging would be left to Thomson.

At this point it should be pointed out that William Thomson (no 'p') was in no way related to John Thompson, the engineer Williams was to dismiss from the *Claymore* in January 1941.

William Thomson went to New Caledonia to charter a ship. By the time he returned to Australia in late March 1941 he had everything in readiness.

The *Niagara*, he argued, had sunk outside of the 'two mile limit' and so was in international waters. His plan was to train two divers in the use of the suit in Australia. A team of seven men would then travel to New Zealand. The ship Thomson had chartered would sail from New Caledonia to the site of the wreck. Here the divers would join it and recover the gold. To avoid the gold being confiscated by the British authorities in New Zealand or Australia the ship would return to New Caledonia. The whole salvage would take three months and cost approximately £4 500. Or so Thomson argued.

To interest investors, Whatmore, Thomson and Uther set out all these details on paper in the form of questions and answers. These questions and answers were produced only weeks after Williams and the *Claymore* crew had found the *Niagara*, yet they contain a remarkable amount of accurate information about a salvage job that was supposedly veiled in secrecy:

Q: How far down in the ocean is the RMS *Niagara*?
A: 60 fathoms.
Q. Location and distance from New Zealand shore of the said wreck in nautical terms?
A: We are reliably informed 4.5 miles off Hen and Chickens Islands.
Q: Is the said wreck properly and accurately marked and/or buoyed at present?
A: We are informed so.
Q: What is the state of ocean currents about the wreck in a general sense?
A: We understand the maximum current is about 1 knot.
Q: Who appears to own or have authority over the wrecked RMS *Niagara* in a legal sense?
A: The underwriters who paid the insurance.
Q: Are you or your representatives legally entitled to salvage or enter the wrecked RMS *Niagara* and on whose authority may you act?
A: Yes. No authority is required.
Q: If you are going to salvage under the Free French Flag is it necessary for your syndicate to get permission of New Zealand, Australian or British Governments to proceed with the salvage operations.
A: The vessel being in extra-territorial waters no such permission would be necessary.

The Thomson-Whatmore-Uther syndicate seemed to have all the answers. At this point, however, in an attempt to assure themselves that they did in fact have a right to salvage the gold and sail away free, they checked some legalities with the Commonwealth Bank in Sydney. The bank promptly contacted Australian Naval Intelligence. The Thomson-Whatmore-Uther syndicate, as well as their sources of information, were about to come under close scrutiny.

* * *

On 2 February, 1941, John Johnstone had been inside the chamber when it had crashed into the side of the *Niagara*. A day later he had been landed successfully on its boat deck before a dragged mooring had the chamber hauled off and bouncing along the seabed. But the *Niagara* had been positively identified, even if it couldn't be determined on which side it lay, and so the *Claymore* returned to Whangarei, in the words of the logbook on 4 February, to: 'Fit the ship for actual salvage work'.

Williams' idea to hold the *Claymore* in position was to use moorings. That is, six heavy mooring blocks would be placed on the seabed in a circle around the *Niagara*. A cable from each block to the surface would be connected to a floating buoy. The *Claymore* would steam into the middle of the circle of mooring blocks, approximately above the *Niagara*. The tender, *Betsy*, would carry a cable from the *Claymore* to the first floating buoy and connect it, then to the second and the third and so on until the *Claymore* was connected to the six mooring blocks by means of six cables. The steam-driven winches on the *Claymore* would pull the cables until the salvage ship was held tight in the middle of its own web of steel cable.

For the mooring blocks on the seabed, Williams had two-ton concrete blocks poured. Additionally, a samson post had to be fitted to the *Claymore* to lift them over the side. For the floating buoys he tried 44 gallon drums held in wooden crates—two drums per buoy.

It took a little over two weeks for the blocks and the other equipment to be made ready. It was not until 18 February, that the *Claymore* proceeded to the wreck. A day was spent using a sounding weight to establish in which direction the *Niagara* lay.

Laying the mooring buoys commenced on 20 February. It did not go successfully and a frustrating week was spent. There were two problems. Firstly, the two ton concrete blocks were not heavy enough to hold the *Claymore* in position and were repeatedly dragged along the seabed. Secondly, when the mooring lines were pulled tight the floating buoys would be pulled underwater to a depth of about 200 feet. At this depth the water pressure crushed the 44-gallon drums.

Williams returned to Whangarei and replaced the drums with casings of World War I mines, which would not crush under the water pressure. He replaced the two-ton mooring blocks with six ton blocks and proceeded to sea again on 2 March, but now found the mine buoys were continually filling up with water and sinking. Again the *Claymore* returned to Whangarei. Williams had the mine buoys tested and found that they leaked in the area where the horns had been removed and the holes welded over. It was another problem that joined his growing list.

*   *   *

The *Orion* had laid 228 mines in the Hauraki Gulf. It laid them on two successive days in two locations. One location was the eastern entrance to the gulf (the Colville Channel) between the mainland and Great Barrier Island; The other was the northern entrance, between Great Barrier Island and Bream Head. After the discovery of the minefield the New Zealand Navy had swept the eastern entrance, sinking eight mines by rifle fire in the process, and so opened the gulf to shipping. The northern entrance, where the *Niagara* had sunk and where the *Claymore* was now working, had not been swept. This was because the Navy had neither the ships nor the personnel which could be relieved from other duties to do the job. The Navy had swept Williams his path to the wreck of the *Niagara*, but had to leave the rest of the northern minefield undisturbed.

Recognising the need to increase its minesweeping fleet the New Zealand Navy requisitioned three ships from private shipping companies to be converted to auxiliary minesweepers. Two of these were the *Gale* and *Puriri*. But the process of requisitioning a ship from a private company, even in a time of war, was a complicated one. The ships had to be inspected, their value determined and a list compiled of everything on board. The private company could protest the requisitioning if it could show that its business, or the New Zealand economy, would suffer as a result of the ship being taken over. Then the ship had to be converted for use as an auxiliary minesweeper, and a crew found to work it. Such proceedings took time. In March 1941, the auxiliary minesweepers commissioned after the *Niagara* sank were still not ready for service.

By this time the mines had been in the water eight months. Many of their moorings had broken loose. Others had moved with the current. Mines began to be washed ashore around the Hauraki Gulf. Fishermen began to watch them float by their fishing boats. And wrestling with the six 800-foot mooring lines that now encircled the *Claymore*, Williams and his crew had their work continually interrupted while someone would be sent in the whaleboat to tie off a mine to a marker buoy so the Navy could be asked to come and get it.

It would still be three months before the clearing of the minefield began in earnest.

SIX

8 March – 29 April 1941

What's That in Those Cases?

By March 1941 Williams was facing yet another problem. Summer was over. The fine days, longer hours of sunlight and relatively clear weather were disappearing. His second trip out to the wreck in March, after the mine buoys were repaired (that is, the leaking areas re-welded) was cut short and the *Claymore* was driven ashore by a storm.

Anchored in the shelter of Urquharts Bay, it must have been a frustrating time for Williams. He had found the *Niagara* six weeks earlier, but one problem after another had prevented sending the observation chamber down to get a clear view of how it lay on the seabed. He must have gone to his bunk still plagued by the problem of how to hold the chamber steady while the *Claymore* rose and fell on the sea's surface. His writing describes what happened next:

Around two o'clock in the morning I woke up, still with the thing thrashing in my mind, when suddenly a light came. A balance weight; and so rig the gear so that each time the ship rolled down to the bell, the slack of its wire would instantly and automatically be picked up, or as the ship rolled the other way, the wire would of itself pay out. Might be the answer! Simple! A lizard block on the wire and a weight on the fall of a roller sheave purchase shackled to the lizard; the weight to run up and down a stay from the masthead, so I got up, drew the thing on a bit of paper, and went down and woke Jim. 'What is it John?' he said and I told him. We poured over it for a few minutes and talked of it, when he said . . . 'We've got all the gear on board and get some sort of weight and try it now: I've had enough of worrying about this one'.

The hands were called and over a cup of tea told the idea. Old Alf [Warren] jumped up in the dim light of the cabin muttering 'that's it, that's it'. Fortunately the ship was rolling and the conditions right for a trial; the gear was rigged in the moonlight then and there and 'out with the bell' weighted as with the diver in it. Over the side it went, and I took the wire around the drum end. The lifting tackle was let go, the wire surged out fast and the bell went down to the bottom, and then up again. One turn only round the winch end and the weight charging up and down the stay and the bell quiet and still in the water, with the ship virtually rolling through its wire.

Perfect! Handles like a toy . . . Dan Scott was now at the winch end in his usual position. And Jim Herd, his eyes sparkling blue, looking at the sun behind me just coming up. Jim Herd, unperturbable, this time shouted, 'By God, she's right' . . . and she was.

We tried her for another couple of hours. Johnstone went in and then his brother, and then the two of them in together. Put the bell on the sand forty fathoms down and there it stayed perfectly still, with its wire taught and holding it upright. Then take her a couple of feet off the bottom, and she was still and quiet again, the occupant undisturbed by the movement of the ship on top.

A counterbalance weight on the rope suspending the observation chamber. It would take up the slack of the rope as the *Claymore* fell with the rolling of the waves, then give out the required slack as it rose. The weight bobbed on its wire attached to the mast and because of this action—of jumping up and down suspended from a wire—the weight, or more correctly the whole device, was referred to from that point on as the 'monkey'.

Williams waited four days for the weather to clear then returned to the *Niagara*. The observation chamber was lowered to the wreck but the visibility was so poor that Bill Johnstone was still unable to report on which side the ship lay. Another storm blew up and the *Claymore* again headed to Urquharts Bay for shelter.

Getting moored up above the *Niagara* became a slow and frustrating process. First Williams would have to wait for the tide before the *Claymore* could be sailed down the river from the Town

Wharf at Whangarei. Then at its top speed of about five knots, the *Claymore* would take four hours to reach the site of the wreck. The job of recovering each of the mooring lines began until the *Claymore* was held fast in the middle of its web. Tying up to the moorings took the crew about two hours. (That was the average time in March. By September, Williams was able to proudly report it was done in a record time of 71 minutes.)

Once above the wreck Williams was reluctant to let go the moorings. This would be done only if coal or water was needed, or the weather became so bad that the *Claymore* was in danger of sinking. Usually the *Claymore* would 'ride it out on the moorings', waiting for the weather to clear so that some useful work could be done. There are various accounts of battling storms while tied to the moorings. One of the most succinct was written by John Johnstone in one of his unpublished manuscripts:

The locals had warned us of what could be expected—little or no notice was taken. The morning we left The Heads was just another of head winds and rough seas.

'I think that we will chance it', said the skipper to James Herd. 'We can tie up to the buoys anyway and hang on. It might clear up'.

The trip out should have been a warning, for with a strong head wind and rough seas, the decks were soon awash the whole way.

'Keep her head into it', but the man at the wheel was finding it more than he could manage at times. The saloon door on the lee side was open and Stanley [Mitchell] insisted that it should remain open. Freddie [Branch—Cook, later replaced by Stan Dianton] had both galley doors bolted from the inside for fear of being washed overboard. In the stokehold 'Nipper' Lowe toiled alone to keep the steam up to the engine room. The engineer was having his share of anxious moments for the antiquated engine groaned in agony.

We had reached the buoys and it was while tying up that the ship must have slewed and got beam on, for a wave swept the decks and through the open saloon door. Water cascaded in torrents, down the stairway, flooding the saloon knee deep. Bad enough in itself, but the water was finding its way into the stokehold. Meanwhile all the mooring lines had been secured.

Below the water continued to pour down and the level was within inches of the boiler fires. At the stern the crew's quarters were flooded, the weight of the water holding down the stern to sea level. The 'bucket brigade' toiled as never before.

I joined the two Skippers on the bridge and listened to them as they discussed their next move.

'I think Jim', said Williams, 'that we will cut away the moorings and go in'.

To this I heard Jim say, 'Do that and you will lose the ship and all hands too'.

I do not think either man had any idea of how things were in the engine room. To have dropped the moorings certainly would have placed the ship in a precarious position. As the engineer said later, 'We did not have enough steam to boil a potato'.

A beam-sea under such conditions, a 'broach to' and the ship would have capsized.

It was midnight before the weather eased and it was decided to make a run for it.

* * *

Just inside the entrance to the Whangarei Harbour is Urquharts Bay and it was to here that the *Claymore* would often head to seek shelter from a storm. Overlooking Urquharts Bay is the Manaia Gardens Guest House and Williams and the crew would often stay there for the night, before continuing up the harbour to Whangarei. Peg Allen, who was staying in the guesthouse with her husband in 1941, wrote to me saying:

One howling stormy night, the tempo of an extraordinary gale reached such a crescendo that we at Manaia Gardens stayed up late, unable to rest, fearing for the safety of the *Claymore* which we knew had been caught out in that open mined sea lane. All felt it would be impossible for them to survive unless they made harbour. Everything was ink-black, trees swaying in the shrieking winds, torrential rains. Suddenly there appeared a faint glow round Home Point at the harbour entrance. Then through the driving rains this circle of light became larger and larger until we recognised a huge blurred light. We all nearly wept with relief. The crew later told us the conditions were so shocking, the only hope of escaping the disaster on that treacherous mountain peaked coast was to find the very narrow harbour entrance by instruments. Miraculously they made it.

*   *   *

On 21 March the *Claymore* again got moored up above the *Niagara*. This time the weather stayed clear long enough for John Johnstone to be successfully lowered four times and clearly identify the wreck. James Herd summarised the situation in a letter to his wife:

Much has happened since I wrote to you last. We left on Friday morning, arrived at our area, moored up over the wreck and sent down the observation chamber but visibility was bad. On Saturday we again sent down the chamber—the day was a perfect one—smooth sea, no wind and everything was excellent for our work. We had four dips and shifted our ship about until the diver landed right where we are to go into the wreck and to our surprise and pleasure the wreck was found to be laying right over on her side and what is more she is laying with her starboard side up, which is the side on which the bullion room is. This means that our work will be much shortened, we have only the shell plating to go through, instead of three decks. There will of course be some deck cutting to be done, but nothing near as much as there would be if she were laying upright. Unfortunately our weather did not last too long. Last night, shortly after we ceased work it commenced to blow like fury. We spent a rotten night, so at daylight this morning we slipped our moorings and ran for shelter.

Discussing the matter of blasting our way into the wreck, John Johnstone is very confident we shall soon accomplish the job. He was so pleased at finding her on her side that he poured over the plans of the ship until 3 o'clock this morning. He has decided where he will place the first shot and how long it will take to blast a hole in the side twenty foot square.

The plans of the *Niagara*, over which Johnstone would have poured showed that the bullion room was 24 feet from the hull plating. They would need to cut through the hull plating itself, the steward's room (which, when the ship had been upright, was beside the bullion room) and across an open hallway.

Then of course they had to enter a sealed room which was approximately 350 feet underwater. A room designed to keep people out, even when it was above water. Williams approached the Union

WHAT'S THAT IN THOSE CASES?

Steam Ship Company for details of the bullion room. But as it had been added after the *Niagara* had been built, its specifications were not in the original plans. The Company replied in a letter saying:

... we are afraid we are unable to supply just what is required. The best we can do is quote from the specifications of [the rooms] construction, as follows: 'A steel room to be built . . . for the storage of bullion. To be constructed of double steel bulkheads, steel floor and ceiling and teak grating on floor. To have a door with two separate Chubb's locks and keys. Latest and best type of burglar alarm'.

Unfortunately there is nothing on the plan to indicate the thickness of the steel.

Williams now had to find a way of blasting a hole in the side of the *Niagara*. His intention was to use gelignite, an explosive made from nitroglycerine, cellulose, nitrate, sodium nitrate and wood pulp. Gelignite was readily available in sticks. That is, the chemicals were combined with the wood pulp in sticks wrapped in heavy waxed paper. Gelignite is exploded by using an electrical detonator.

For his purposes, Williams purchased ten tons of gelignite. This caused some consternation in Whangarei and Williams was asked not to store the explosive in the town. He decided to hide it on one of the islands in the Hen and Chickens group. Arthur Bryant was given the task:

Captain Williams said to me 'Right, well you go and pick a site where this is to be stored'. We took it out to the Hen and Chickens and on one of the Chickens a little creek ran up the slope. Well I walked along and on the side of the hill right in line with a point was quite a nice big tree. And I walked along until I got that in line with the peak and I walked into the scrub a few yards and there we made our stockpile.

Testing of the explosives began on 6 April. Sticks of gelignite were sewn inside canvas tubes along with an electrical detonator. The tube was weighted and lowered under water. Two wires to the detonator were touched to a car battery and the gelignite exploded. That is, when it was about 60 feet underwater. Any deeper and it began to misfire. The detonator would explode, but the gelignite wouldn't, as the logbook reports: 'Wires connected . . . shot fired, detonators exploded but shot failed to go off. Frame and shot hoisted on board for examination, gelatine still in canvas saving at ends where the explosion of the detonator had apparently blown out'.

John Johnstone contacted someone he knew at Nobels of London, the company formed by the Swedish inventor of dynamite (and after whom the Nobel Prize is named). He received a reply that there was no knowledge of explosives at such a depth.

The problems persisted for weeks. Different containers were tried for the gelignite. It was put in tins and lengths of household drainpipe. The detonator was inserted and sealed using different methods. Some ideas worked at greater depths than others, but none worked at 350 feet.

* * *

While the experiments with explosives continued, so did the problems with mooring the *Claymore* over the wreck. The World War I mine buoys were still not satisfactory. They would repeatedly, and unexpectedly, spring a leak, fill with water and sink.

It was some time in the middle of April that someone suggested to Williams that he consider kauri logs for his mooring buoys. The logbook makes no mention of it, but Johnstone's movie film shows Williams and three other men, all dressed in suits, at the base of a giant kauri tree, while James Herd's diary of 15 April records: 'Today we took on board two lengths of kauri log to try out as buoys— hope they're successful'.

The kauri (pronounced cow-ree) pine of New Zealand is a truly remarkable tree. Mature kauris have been discovered which are 3 000 years old. They reach over 100 feet high and have a trunk diameter of over 10 feet. Importantly, the trunk of the kauri will reach 80 or 100 feet straight up before sprouting branches. Such lengths of straight timber, without knots, were prized by the Maori people for use as canoes and a visitor to the Bay of Islands in 1820 described such canoes: 'The largest we saw was 84 feet long, six feet wide and five feet deep. It was made of a single cowry (kauri) tree hollowed out. The chief sat at the stern and steered the canoe, which was impelled by the force of ninety naked men.'

The European sailors who began to visit the north island of New Zealand soon recognised the value of the kauri for ships' masts and began trading with the Maoris. After European settlement the kauri proved to have the widest commercial value of any tree and contributed to the pioneering economy of the colony. The forests of this magnificent tree were devastated, as trees that mature over centuries cannot be replaced in a generation. Today in New Zealand any giant kauri still standing (usually in the less accessible mountain regions) is individually named, registered and protected.

In 1941, however, such protection was still not in place and Williams was able to purchase a giant kauri with a diameter of approximately five feet. The trunk was cut into six-foot lengths and the sections shaped. The light pine wood had the buoyancy to suspend 400 feet of cable going down to the concrete mooring blocks on the seabed. When pulled 200 feet underwater, the solid pine would not crush.

Another problem was solved during this period. That was the problem of the chamber spinning as it descended and ascended. This was solved by plaiting three ropes to form one. No one understood why, but when the chamber was lowered on the plaited rope the violent spinning was reduced to a very slow 'winding up' of about twelve turns by the time the wreck was reached. On the ascent the chamber would slowly revolve the other way, unwinding itself. Twelve revolutions was considered manageable and the plaited rope was used during the remainder of the salvage.

Experiments with the explosives continued until the logbook reports on 22 April: 'proceeding towards Whangarei to obtain water pipes and if possible some form of electrical connection which will enable firing to be done after the tube has been hermetically sealed'.

Now the gelignite was put inside two-inch water pipe. Cordite was added before the detonator, then a plate welded over the end. Two small holes were drilled in the end plate to allow the wires from the detonator to protrude. The cordite (yet another chemical cousin of gelignite and dynamite) was added to aid detonation.

Tests were made which appeared successful. Explosive tubes made from the water pipes were submerged to 120 feet, left for two hours and then detonated. There was nothing on the end of the rope to bring to the surface.

On 25 April the first attempt to lay a shot on the side of the *Niagara* was made. Eighteen pounds of gelignite was put inside a length of water pipe along with cordite and a detonator. Johnstone went down in the chamber to guide the explosive tube into position. At 11.10 a.m. the shot was in place and the chamber brought to the surface.

The wires connected to the detonator were touched to the car battery and a thump was felt through the deck of the *Claymore* which broke crockery in the saloon and had rivets popping out of the rusting hull. A hundred yards in every direction dead fish floated to the surface.

Johnstone got back in the chamber and was lowered to the wreck. In his notebook he made a sketch of the result. A section of the hull plating, some twenty feet in length had been loosened on the side of the *Niagara*.

The *Claymore* returned to Whangarei again. The addition of cordite to aid detonation, along with sealed waterpipe containers, seemed to have solved the problem. But cordite was not freely available, so while the crew set about making waterpipe containers, Williams drove to Auckland to purchase guncotton (cotton soaked in nitric acid) from the Naval Base. Guncotton is particularly volatile and under certain conditions (heat, dryness) will explode if merely bumped.

Williams bought eight cases of guncotton and stacked them on the back seat of his car. He then bought some cases of detonators which he stacked on the roof and set off to drive back to Whangarei. He recalled that as the Auckland ferry was nearing the North Shore a policeman, who was also on the ferry, came across and asked 'What's on top of the car?' Then looking in the back seat said, 'And in God's name what's that in those cases?'

'Guncotton', Williams replied. 'And detonators on the roof'.

Williams then explained what he was doing. When the ferry reached the shore the policeman said quietly, 'Look mister, get going and for Christ's sake don't tell anyone you saw me'.

As he drove off, Williams heard the policeman call, 'And good luck'.

WHAT'S THAT IN THOSE CASES?

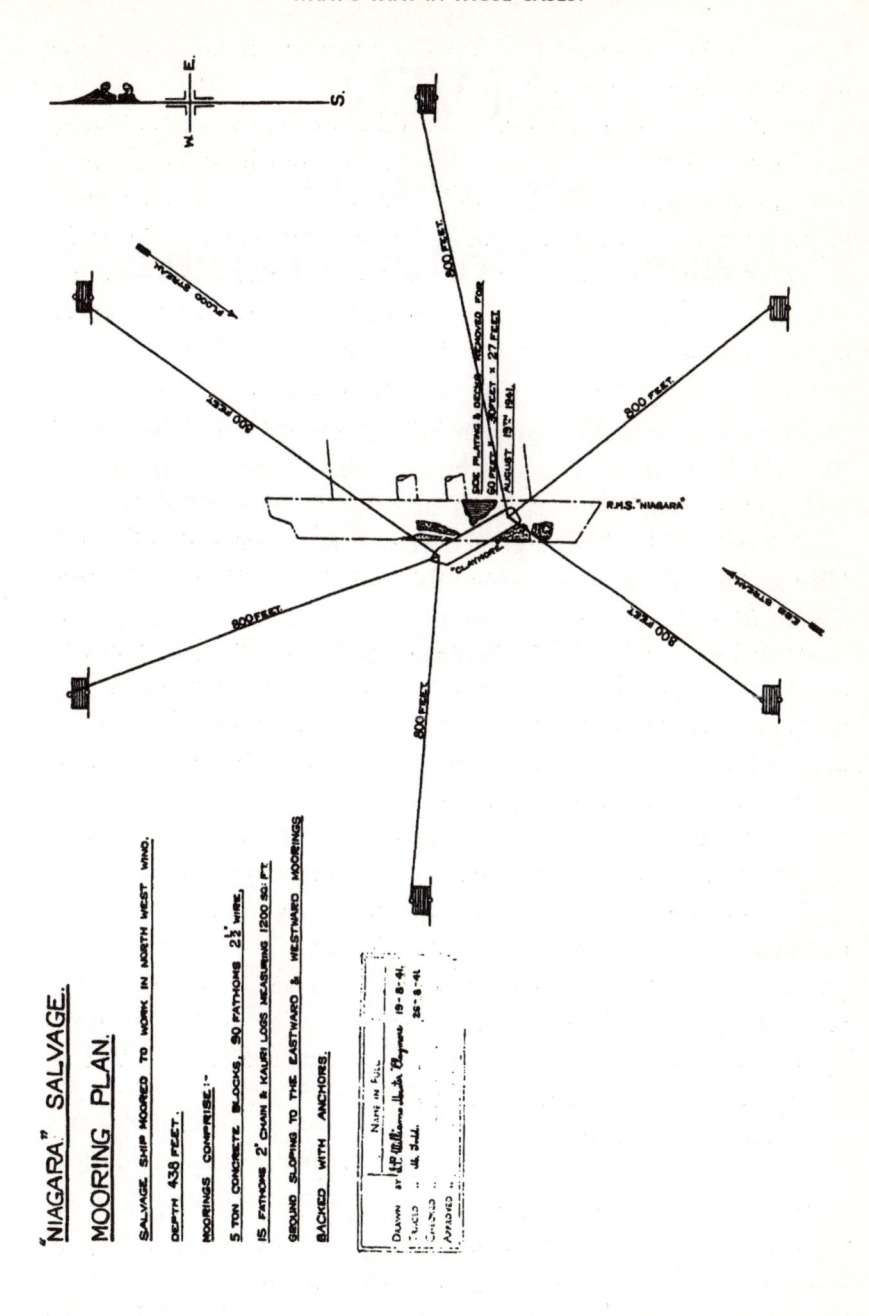

Williams drawing of the mooring plan showing the mooring blocks encircling the wreck and the *Claymore* anchored above it.

SEVEN

30 April – 20 July 1941

Winter Is On Us in Earnest

After he had sent the dissenting crew members, Thompson and Paulson, back to Australia in January, Williams replaced them with first and second engineers hired in New Zealand. These had not proved satisfactory. They argued over their responsibilities. They also threatened to bring the salvage to the notice of the Seamen's Union, saying the *Claymore* was unsafe, the work dangerous and that the crew were not being paid overtime for the long hours they were working. Williams fired one of them. The other lost the top joint of a finger while working the reversing gear on the engine. He was sent to hospital and not asked to rejoin the crew when he recovered. Williams now cabled one of his partners in the United Salvage Syndicate in Australia to send across an Australian Chief Engineer.

Jim Kemp joined the *Claymore* at the end of April 1941 and was the fourth and final crew member I was to find still living. He told me how he was invited to join the salvage:

I was the Deputy Superintendent Engineer with the AUSN Company and the Managing Partner, Mr Donald McKay of McDonald Hamilton, called for me to discuss an unknown mission. He wouldn't tell me what the mission was. He said it was a salvage job in New Zealand and the only thing he could do was to give me a copy of *Egypt's Gold* by David Scott, which he said would give me some idea of what type of salvage it was. At that stage I didn't know the *Niagara* had been mined, nor did I know it was carrying gold. But any rate I was told to read the book that night and come in the following morning and give him my answer, whether I would go or not.

I did [agree to go] the following morning.

I was given a ticket to Auckland on a fast passenger ship with a Naval escort, and I went over. I arrived in Auckland and caught a train up to Whangarei. The first time I heard of the salvage of the *Niagara*'s gold was when I was sitting in the hotel in Whangarei. I also heard a description of the *Claymore*, which didn't please me very much. But from then on I was a member of the crew.

Later on I found that was most important, the fact that I was not engaged specifically to do work on a salvage ship over the *Niagara*, in a minefield. And it became one of the reasons that we had salvage rights.

*   *   *

The history of British salvage law dates from 1275, when Edward I's Statute of Westminster restricted the right of the Crown to unclaimed wrecks only. Prior to that any wreck, whether claimed or not, had been considered the property of the King.

A more specific law was introduced in 1353. The Crown's rights of jurisdiction over unclaimed wrecks on the high seas were granted to the British Admiralty. Simultaneously, wrecks washed ashore came under local jurisdiction. This unfortunately led to the practice of wrecking ships on certain areas of the British coastline to claim the wreck or its cargo. It was not until 1753 that George II made it a felony to put out false lights to lure ships onto rocks, or to 'beat, wound or obstruct' people trying to escape from foundering vessels. In 1809 George III legislated against sailors cutting ships cables so that they could loot ships that went ashore after being cast adrift.

The British Admiralty, charged as it was in 1353, with the responsibility of arbitrating in cases of salvage rights, recognised the importance of encouraging sailors to attempt to save a ship and its cargo, rather than stand by and see it founder, or worse, actively help wreck it. The Admiralty Court arbitrated on many cases over the centuries, giving a reward to salvors who successfully saved or recovered a ship or its cargo. The size of the reward is arbitrary, but tradition says it should not be more than half the value. When considering the size of the reward the Admiralty Court usually took into consideration the value of the cargo or ship salved and the degree of personal risk encountered.

Salvage jurisdiction was formally consolidated in Admiralty Courts in 1894 by the *Merchant Shipping Act*.

In 1941 the rights of crews in regards to salvage were covered by this Act. I quote from a letter that Williams received on the matter some six months after completing work on the *Niagara*:

> The fact that the men had been engaged for salvage work, and were being paid wages accordingly, would no doubt be taken into consideration by the court fixing the amounts of the awards, but would not in any way affect their right to the same. The principal factors in fixing the aggregate amount to be awarded would doubtless be (a) the value of the property salved and (b) the degree of personal risk and exertion involved on the part of the Masters and crews.

A further quote from the *Merchant Shipping Act* of 1894 seems relevant:

> 156. - (1) a seaman . . . shall not by any agreement . . . abandon any right that he may have or obtain in the nature of the salvage; and every stipulation in any agreement inconsistent with any provision of this Act shall be void.

* * *

With the arrival of Jim Kemp to take over the responsibilities of chief engineer in late April, Williams now had a crew on board the *Claymore* that would remain basically unchanged. This crew was as follows:

J. P. (John) Williams - master
J. (James) Herd - chief salvage officer
J. E. (John) Johnstone - chief diver
W. (Bill) Johnstone - diver
J. H. (Jim) Kemp - chief engineer
A. W. (Alf) Warren - engineer
W. J. (Joe) Alcock - second mate
A. J. (Arthur) Bryant - fireman
S. (Stan) Mitchell - steward
W. (Bill) Green - able seaman
N. G. (Nipper) Lowe - able seaman
L. (Les) Mischewski - ship's boy

T. (Tommy) Nalder – able seaman
R. S. (Ray) Nelson – able seaman
S. (Stan) Dianton – cook
R. (Bluey) Rigby – able seaman

The first ten names (with the exceptions of James Herd and Jim Kemp) formed the team that originally travelled from Australia. The last six are all New Zealanders and joined Williams in Auckland or Whangarei.

After having many men leave the *Claymore* for various reasons, from having other commitments to refusing to work in a minefield, Williams himself was pleased to finally have the situation become stable. Some weeks after Jim Kemp joined, Williams expressed his satisfaction in a letter to an associate in Melbourne:

We now have a first-class crew on deck, when we are at sea that is. In port they seem to have established an enviable reputation for getting drunk, fighting the locals and generally earning a name for themselves and the ship. We are only at the town wharf about once every ten days and then only for a few hours and they work right on with no weekends or time off. They are entitled to have the time off for their particular form of amusement. I may say their looks suit their behaviour.

Perhaps Williams was trying to paint a romantic picture of a happy, tight-knit band of pirates sharing an adventure. Working hard and playing hard together. The recollections and evidence indicate a different story, however. They were men separated by age, experience and outlook. When the *Claymore* was in Whangarei the crew were usually happy to be relieved of the confines of the ship and go their own ways and were often unaware what the others were doing. Arthur Bryant's fiancée travelled from Australia and the two were married during the salvage. Yet fellow crew member Ray Nelson did not know of this until I told him 50 years later.

Williams would spend time with his wife and family. James Herd would sometimes stay with them. The young New Zealanders, joined by Billy Green, drank and chased girls. The Johnstone brothers would stay with the friends they had made in Whangarei.

Others would go to the movies. Tommy Nalder, who had joined the crew in Auckland, met his future wife at the milk bar next to the Plaza Theatre.

Arthur Bryant recalled there was a dance school and tracing the owners I received a letter from Mrs Thora Danaher (née Warrington), which in part, read:

We had a big dancing school called the Warrington School of Dancing where my sister and I taught. I was the ballroom and tap specialist and my sister Claudia highland and ballet. There was a billiard room upstairs above the studio and the boys from the *Claymore* used to go there a lot and being cheeky used to open the studio door and give us all sorts of cheek and as time went by we got to know them, and any parties that the studio had, they were invited.

I remember we put on a big party for the crew and I think nearly all of Whangarei attended. Champagne was flowing by the case. I remember rescuing a bottle, which I still have, with the names of the crew on the label which I got them to write. I have still got this bottle at home and have kept it all these 50 years.

A photo of my sister in her kilts with all her trophies used to be on the wall in the studio. I believe it was taken by one of the crew and hung in the *Claymore*. Where it is now I wouldn't know.

* * *

By the beginning of May 1941, the initial enthusiasm for the adventure must have been wearing thin. Winter was approaching, and the crew faced months of gruelling, cold, monotonous work in uncomfortable, cramped conditions. Jim Kemp recalled that the first thing he did upon joining the *Claymore* was to put three inches of cement on the floor of his cabin to stop the sea water flowing through. He also recalled that the food was less than desirable.

'We had no refrigeration and meat was kept in a meat safe over the stern of the *Claymore* and after about eight days you wouldn't go near the stern of the *Claymore*. And you certainly wouldn't eat the meat'.

James Herd wrote to his wife:

. . . everyday we learn something. First we found the method of locating the ship. In the Egypt job it took the Italians three years to find their job. Then we found the way to moor our ship, then we found the wreck on her side, although this gave us cause for a lot of worry until we eventually found that she was right over on her [port] side. We then found we could place our shots just where we wanted them, all these things we found by experiment, but we can't find anywhere or anyway to overcome the weather.

*   *   *

At the same time, in Australia, the Whatmore-Thomson-Uther salvage expedition needed finance. How they came to make themselves known to Sidney Davis I do not know. But Davis was approached to invest £5 000 in the salvage. To check if they could legitimately attempt to salvage the gold Davis had his accountant (W. F. Austin) approach the Commonwealth Bank with the details. The bank's memorandum following the meeting records:

...Mr W. F. Austin called concerning the *Niagara*. Mr Austin advised he was an accountant and that he had been consulted by his client Mr S. H. Davis, who had been approached by the syndicate controlling the new diving suit with a suggestion that he invest £5 000 in their proposal to salvage gold from the *Niagara*.

The main person interested in the diving suit appears to be Mr Henry Whatmore, Solicitor. A Mr W. H. Thomson is also closely interested.

Mr Austin quoted accurate figures of the amount of gold on the *Niagara* and further stated that is was South African gold, the property of the Bank of England, handled by the Commonwealth Bank as agents. He also stated that he was aware from information received from New Zealand, that a salvage vessel manned by Melbourne people, had been over the wreck for some time and that this vessel was using a diving bell.

Austin returned to the Commonwealth Bank five days later, this time accompanied by the proposed investor, Sidney Davis. Austin and Davis, it appears, no longer planned to invest in the Whatmore–Thomson–Uther salvage attempt, but to make an attempt of their own. After this meeting the bank's memorandum records:

Messrs Austin and Davis then stated that Mr Davis had decided not to join in the proposed effort by Messrs Whatmore and Thomson but proposed to form a syndicate of his own called 'The Right to Search the *Niagara*

Syndicate' or something similar. From the conversation I gathered the opinion that they considered the persons at present controlling the diving suit were not sufficiently strong financially to carry the venture to a successful conclusion and that Mr Davis hoped ultimately to acquire at his own price the rights to the diving suit, and then attempt salvage operations with official concurrence—i.e. they hope we will seek their assistance if our present efforts are unsuccessful. The impression they left was that they were doubtful as to the success of our own present operation, and that they have some confidence in the new diving suit.

The Davis-Austin plan appears to have been to discredit Whatmore and Thomson, buy the rights to the suit from them cheaply, wait for Williams and the *Claymore* crew to fail at their task, then step in and using the anti-paralysis suit get the gold for the bank.

The Commonwealth Bank passed this information onto Military Intelligence who thoroughly investigated everyone involved, imposed censorship on them and proceeded to: 'do everything possible to define the syndicate and its operations with a view to restraining them from doing anything which might be detrimental to the national resources'.

Whatmore, Thomson, Austin and Davis had their phones tapped, their incoming and outgoing international mail opened and read, their bank accounts audited. Their passports were flagged and any application to leave the country was to be referred to Military Intelligence. Additionally, their backgrounds were thoroughly checked.

The other salvage plans for the gold in the *Niagara* were effectively stopped from that point on. But the mystery of how they obtained their information remained.

In an interview conducted on 18 April 1941 Henry Whatmore said, 'It was Lieutenant-Commander Wilkinson who first gave us the information that there was bullion on the *Niagara*'.

In response to this, Wilkinson replied in a report to his superiors saying:

. . . I in no way either stated or implied that there was bullion in the ship;

it is extremely doubtful whether even the *Niagara* was mentioned but I am prepared to accept this as a possibility.

So far as I can recall the conversations, I discussed the suit in general and asked whether it were still available. I was informed that the essential portions of the suit were available but that certain hose lines, compressor etc would have to be supplied and that the trained diver Childs, was away in HMAS *Australia*. The depth of 60 fathoms would have been mentioned in discussion of [the] compressor required. There was no occasion to mention either *Niagara* or bullion.

Even if (which seems unlikely) the second salvage syndicate learnt from Wilkinson that there was gold bullion aboard the *Niagara*, it still does not explain how they were to also learn, with such accuracy, about the position and depth of the wreck, progress regarding the salvage, that a diving chamber was being used and other such information.

Neither were the Australian Navy able find the informant. The best it could do was offer another possibility, which the Director of Naval Intelligence, Commander R. B. M. (Cocky) Long, did in his report to the Director, Security Service, dated 4 June 1941:

It has been reliably reported that on at least two occasions a Mrs Campbell who recently arrived from New Zealand and who is now residing at St Kilda Road, Melbourne, has stated in public that there is bullion in the wreck of the RMS *Niagara* and that the source of her information was Mrs Williams, wife of Captain Williams who is at present conducting operations for salvage of the bullion.

A point that Naval Intelligence didn't pick up on, however, was that Sidney Davis (the investor) was the nephew of Sir Ernest Davis, the Mayor of Auckland. Sir Ernest socialised with Williams while the *Claymore* was being fitted out in Auckland and his private yacht was regularly reported in the Hauraki Gulf.

But in April 1941, with what they considered a satisfactory explanation, and with the second salvage attempt both discredited and effectively thwarted, the Australian Navy now considered the matter closed.

* * *

On the *Claymore* the work continued lowering explosives to the side of the *Niagara* and detonating them . . . a process hampered by the condition of the *Claymore*, the constant shifting of the mooring blocks, the tangling of mooring lines and the deteriorating weather. The underwater explosions also put a strain on the hull of the *Claymore*.

'Our hull was made of lomore iron', Jim Kemp told me, 'but in some places it was paper thin. It was so thin that we couldn't bolt or rivet anything to it. We had to put a sandwich plate on each side and squeeze up the old plate in between with sheets of rubber insertions'.

On one occasion a large piece of rusted hull, below the waterline, collapsed and water began pouring in. The *Claymore* was moored over the wreck with no chance of making it to shore. Heavy objects were put into the lifeboat, which was then swung out on the samson post on the opposite side to the leak. The *Claymore* heeled over until the hole came clear of the water. The hole was repaired, the water bucketed out, the lifeboat swung inboard and work resumed.

On 12 May it started to blow a gale and the *Claymore* began dragging its moorings. Jim Kemp takes up the story:

During the night it blew up a gale and we took off down the Hauraki Gulf and our moorings with us. These moorings were most valuable. We had to build them—had to pour the concrete block—you could not get anything in the war time. So whenever we dragged one we never ever lost it. We never let it go. We stayed with it until we stopped. But on this night we stopped at about 4 a.m. and pulled up with a dead jerk and tried to get it up and it wouldn't move. It came up a little way and it wouldn't move any further.

So we turned in until daylight, tried again and the same thing happened. It would not come any further than about 50 feet from the surface. So we put Johnno down in his diving suit and lo and behold we'd lifted the Trans-Pacific [Telephone] Cable off the bottom. So we put a shackle around the cable and took the weight of it and released the mooring and gently lowered the cable back and never, ever told anyone about it.

On the morning of 13 May, while the *Claymore* crew were

A postcard of the RMS *Niagara*. When it was launched it was described as 'the Titanic of the Pacific'.

The front cover of the RMS *Niagara*'s on board newspaper, 'The Niagara News'.

John Williams (above left) and James Herd (above right) talking to the diver in the observation chamber.

Diver John Johnstone (left) dressed in a traditional 'hard hat' diving suit.

Bill Johnstone, who insisted on wearing his Australian Navy cap during the entire expedition.

Amid a maze of ropes and wires the observation chamber is suspended over the side of the *Claymore*.

Arthur Bryant pushes down on the plunger to detonate an underwater explosive charge.

The underwater observation chamber as it stands in the Market Museum, Castlemaine, Victoria.

The *Claymore*, held in place by the mooring lines, above the wreck.

The crew celebrate the recover of the first gold in the saloon of the *Claymore*. Standing at the rear from left to right are: Tommy Nalder (with piano accordion), Billy Green, 'Nipper' Lowe, Victor Neilley, Stan Mitchell, Bill Johnstone, Jim Kemp and Les Mischewski. Sitting around the table from left to right are: Unknown, Ray Nelson, Stan Dianton, Danny Scott (partly obscured), James Herd, John Williams, John Johnstone (holding gold), Alf Warren, James Taylor, Arthur Bryant and Joe Alcock

John Johnstone (left) and John Williams remove bars of gold from boxes on the deck of the *Claymore*.

The crew pose for a photograph around a pile of gold stacked on a bulkhead of the *Claymore*.

144 bars, almost two tons of gold, stacked on the floor of the Whangarei Branch of the Bank of New Zealand. This is a little over one quarter of the total recovered.

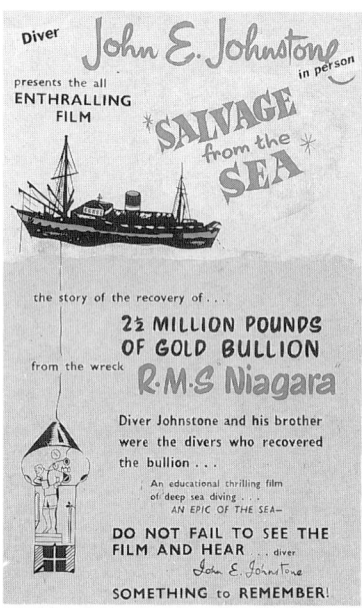

A poster for John Johnstone's silent film which he showed during the 1950's and 1960's.

John Johnstone climbs into the 'iron man suit' aboard the *Foremost 17* in 1953.

untangling one of their mooring blocks from the Trans-Pacific Telephone Cable, a few miles to the north the fishing boat *Pearline* caught a mine in its fishing net. It attached a float buoy to the mine and net, then radioed the New Zealand Navy which sent the patrol boat *Rawea* to the area.

Commander J. E. Briton, RNVR, in command of the *Rawea* was later questioned by a Naval Board of Enquiry as to what happened when he approached the mine. The report of the board records him saying:

All we could see was the buoy on the surface. I kept my ship well away and called for a volunteer to come with me in the ship's boat to investigate. I approached the buoy and raised 30 feet of new manilla two inch line which had come to the surface fairly easily. The mine then came into view. Up to this stage we were not sure whether the *Pearline* had mistaken it for one of the old contact mines the *Claymore* used for buoys for her moorings and which had broken adrift on numerous occasions.

The mine stopped, sat about six foot below the surface and from that we gathered it was still attached to the moorings and had been dragged into the shallow water by the fishing boat. It appeared to be a moored mine . . . similar to the others that had been swept.

I then sent a message to the Naval Officer in Charge, Auckland, requesting the assistance of a sweeper.

The newly commissioned auxiliary minesweepers *Gale* and *Puriri* were sent from Auckland to deal with the mine. They spent the night of 13 May anchored in Urquharts Bay, alongside the *Claymore*. At the Naval Board of Enquiry, the Commander of the Gale (Lieutenant Commander Cathel McLeod, RNVR) was asked to describe what happened at daybreak on 14 May:

I picked up anchor a few minutes before the *Puriri* and on the way out met the *Rawea* coming in and had some conversation with her concerning the mine and she said it might be only about three feet under the water. I carried on towards the position 053 [degrees] 8.5 miles from Bream Head. Before I arrived there I did notice that the *Puriri* was following and I was not surprised because it was a very bad day for sweeping.

I did not give any orders after that as I thought the *Puriri* might be helpful in finding the mine. As I could not see the buoy marking the mine I shaped a course two miles to the northward of the position where it should have been. I went to this position taking care to keep clear of the minefield. I then turned around and steered 180 degrees. The *Puriri* followed behind on our port quarter.

McLeod then explained how he searched unsuccessfully for the mine, the *Puriri* following him.

Question: How did you fix your position?
Answer: I fixed it on the Westerly end of the Hen and the Easterly end of the Chicken.
Question: What then happened?
Answer: I was going round in that circle very slowly and I had just completed a quarter of that circle when the *Puriri* blew up.
Question: What did you do when the *Puriri* blew up?
Answer: I put the helm hard to starboard and went full speed ahead to go to her assistance. The *Puriri* must have been a mile away from us at the time she blew up and I think she must have altered her course to the westward five or ten minutes previous to that.

The bow section of the *Puriri* had been blown off. It sank within seconds. Five men died, five were injured, the remainder of the crew of 22 were unhurt. After the Board of Enquiry, held two days later, the New Zealand Navy resolved to clear the minefield.

Until this time a total of twenty mines (including two that sank the *Niagara* and one that sank the *Puriri*) had been accounted for. The Navy was not to know that there were still 208 somewhere in the Hauraki Gulf. It commenced clearing the minefield on 13 June 1941, exactly one year after the *Orion* had laid it.

* * *

It was six months since the *Claymore* had begun its search for the *Niagara* and in his report to the bank, Williams wrote:

Now that Winter is on us in earnest the whole thing has developed into a battle with the weather. When there is much sea or swell we cannot work with the grab as the sudden rising of the ship brings her whole weight on the gear and we have had several escapes from bringing it down about our ears. I feel however that we now really have the job well in hand and it is simply a matter of waiting for the weather fine enough to work in.

When the Navy commenced clearing the minefield Williams had another interruption—the explosion of mines. The minesweepers were working all around the *Claymore* and for them to detonate a mine in close proximity, while the observation chamber was underwater, could mean the loss of the chamber and the death of the diver. Such an explosion occurred on 22 June when John Johnstone was in the chamber. The mine was less than a mile away and its detonation 'rattled my teeth and sent the instruments haywire', as Johnstone put it.

The *Claymore* returned to Whangarei and while the boiler was being repaired Williams was summoned to Auckland by the naval authorities to discuss the situation. It was agreed that the *Claymore* would suspend a black ball from its mast while the chamber was underwater. When a minesweeper in the area was about to sink a mine it would signal the *Claymore* with a light, then not commence firing at the mine until the ball was lowered.

The observation chamber had now completed over 100 dives to depths of around 400 feet. Concerned about fatigue in the metal and glass, as well as the effects of the bumping and underwater explosions, Williams wrote to David Isaacs, the designer of the chamber. Isaacs replied in a letter dated 17 July:

. . . the observation chamber being used off New Zealand has (a) been underwater during blasting operations (b) suffered considerable dragging underwater with consequent denting and general damage.

The following seems pertinent.

Blasting underwater must produce an effect akin to depth charges in relation to submarines. While it may be possible to inflict a slight degree of damage on the metal work of the observation chamber . . . it must be remembered that the glass windows, under repeated submersion and blows due to blasting, may suffer fatigue and give way suddenly . . . and under the conditions of external pressure which are operating, the stress conditions may then become unstable. Collapse would then be sudden and complete.

When I designed the observation chamber I naturally had in mind a certain amount of ill treatment . . . but was not led to believe there would be conditions of operation such that the chamber would become to any degree battered about. I wish to make it clearly understood that this chamber may become actually dangerous to the occupant if it is operated while obviously suffering from any degree of denting.

The observation chamber was designed for submergence to 600 feet for an indefinitely large number of times, but the thickest and best glass obtainable was not good enough for these conditions. Actually, as far as was known when the observation chamber was designed, it was to be used for depths around 350 feet, and I therefore had no hesitation in using the glass at present installed. The present position however is that with the increase in depth to 450 feet the stresses in the glass are to my mind getting fairly high.

Williams' initial report to the Commonwealth Bank of Australia had estimated that the salvage would take six months and 'charter of vessel, insurance, wages, stores, bunkers, etc.' would cost the bank £27 800. Financially he was well under budget. But it was taking longer than expected and many members of the crew (who had signed six-month work contracts) were now considering leaving. In a letter to G. M. Shain, the Commonwealth Bank official with whom he had originally negotiated the salvage contract, Williams wrote:

When I engaged the Australian crew in Melbourne I promised them a certain weekly wage in lieu of overtime, and a bonus if the venture succeeded, with the object first, of making them, as far as possible, thus feel that they were sharers in all that was being done, and also because, by so doing I hoped to get away from the danger of Union interference.

The seamen's award contains clauses dealing with salvage work; it is almost an axiom that high rates are paid and I realised that if the Unions ever came into it, not only would the expense be enormous, but the interference intolerable, in such work as this.

After I left, the men signed an agreement for their weekly pay which stated that it was to include overtime etc. They spoke to me about it and I reaffirmed my promise to them about the bonus.

When the New Zealand men were taken on the position again arose and, to hold those whom we had trained and who were worthwhile, I made a similar promise to them as well. In neither case, at the time, did I specify any particular definite sum.

During the winter when our fortunes were at their lowest ebb, the question was raised again, and realising that something would have to be done, I promised the men a definite sum of so much for each box brought to the surface, according to their rank on board. At the time one of the Australians had announced his intention of taking his discharge when the term was up; I could have well done without him but realised his defection might very easily spread to others and bring things to a stop. To have said that I would refer the matter to Melbourne would have been useless, and as I have felt myself quite free throughout, to pay such wages and make such arrangements as best suited me, having in mind the limit placed on the expenditure as a whole, I thought little more about it, feeling that if the gold was not won it would not matter, and if it was, I had acted well within my authority, since the bonus was definitely in lieu of overtime and salvage conditions generally.

Williams had to make a specific offer to ensure the crew would stay on until the completion of the job, estimated at the time to be another three months. Total expenses met by the bank at this point were around £15 000. Even if the salvage were to continue another six months Williams was confident he could complete it and still pay the men a bonus and keep the budget under £28 000. The offer to the men was that they would share among them an amount of £28 5s. 0d. per box of gold (each box containing two bars). Even if all gold was recovered the bonus would amount to a modest £7 773 15s. 0d. (Plus the £3 000 promised to John Johnstone).

*   *   *

Through the June and July the tedious work of blasting a way into the wreck continued. Few changes were made to the equipment. The only improvement to the underwater explosives was made at the suggestion of Jim Kemp:

I came up with the idea of cutting a slot along the bottom of each pipe, to make them blow downward with the full pressure. Because blasting gelatine blows downwards, always in water. Doesn't matter if it's two or three feet or 400. We reduced the thickness of the tube to about a sixteenth of an inch in contact with the steel [of the hull]. Then we could cut like a guillotine.

Only John and Bill Johnstone, watching the hole widen in the *Niagara*, could see the progress being made. The rest of the crew could do no more than watch the rope that suspended the chamber disappear beneath the surface, then obediently work at their particular task as Williams spoke into the telephone to the diver.

While the chamber and grab were operating on the wreck the crew were working with what would appear to be a tangled mess of wires and ropes: 500 feet of plaited rope to the chamber, another 500 feet of telephone cable, the wire to lower the explosives, the three wires that controlled the grab. Then there were the six mooring lines that each went 800 feet to the mooring blocks on the seabed.

Each line was raised or lowered, lengthened or shortened by means of one of the three steam-driven winches.

From his wooden chair positioned on the bridge deck, where he sat speaking on the telephone, Williams would orchestrate the clutter.

'Lower the bell. Lower the grab'.

The forward winch suspending the grab, and the winch in the hold of the after deck (it was in the hold simply because there wasn't the space for it on the deck) would be engaged by levers and begin turning slowly while the chamber and grab would disappeared beneath the water.

'Stop the bell. Stop the grab'.

Williams would listen carefully to the telephone, while one of the Johnstone brothers peered through a porthole four inches in diameter to make out the green-blue shape of the area of the wreck where they were suspended.

'Slack the fo'ard mooring'

And the *Claymore* would move a few feet with the current.

'Stop. Open the grab'.

More hissing of steam. More steel cable being unwound from a winch drum.

'Lower the grab. Close the grab'.

A wait while Williams listened into the telephone. A muffled curse and a shake of the head.

'Missed it. Open the grab'.

And the massive steel jaws of the grab, which weighed over a ton, would creak open underwater and prepare to take another bite at the sunken passenger liner.

Witnesses who saw the *Claymore* crew in action in the later months of the salvage repeatedly remarked that they were unable to understand how the crew members, positioned as they were in different places, were able to coordinate their activities with such precision that it appeared as if they were controlled by a sixth sense.

John Johnstone made a cardboard model of the side of the *Niagara*. It was kept on display on the *Claymore* and after a section of the hull had been torn away, Johnstone would tear away the corresponding section of cardboard on the model. The crew could follow the progress of the demolition.

Sometimes a length of the hull plating would be blown loose and the jaws of the grab would take hold of it in an attempt to tear it off. When the piece of plating was firmly caught in the jaws the grab would be wound in, heeling the *Claymore* over until the starboard deck would be down to the water. The *Claymore* would rise and fall on the swell, tugging at the piece of plating. Sometimes it tore free. Sometimes the grab would need to let go its prize as the *Claymore* was in danger of capsizing or some piece of the equipment would be damaged. In a letter to his wife, James Herd wrote:

We are making good progress but the grabbing is slow. When we get hold of a large piece of plating our ship heels right over down to her rails, the water comes up on the decks and we have to let it go. We then put down a shot and break up the plate, then have another go at the grabbing and so it goes on. The grabbing is very monotonous work and we rarely haul anything to the surface, it is far too slow, we simply make a grab and when it bites and holds anything we heave it clear of the wreck, haul off a few feet and let it go, heave back again and go on grabbing. This goes on all day, but as we can't see what we are doing it gets monotonous, but it's good to know we are making progress.

By early June a large section of both A and B decks was cleared away. The deck immediately above the bullion room now began to receive the explosive charges. In his monthly report to the bank, Williams wrote:

Since I last wrote to you we have not got much further. First of all because we are having a lot of bother with a section of C-deck which has folded down over the one below and secondly I have had to stop work while the minesweepers have been clearing the area, once more, of mines. Curiously enough they have swept up a great number and as we felt the blast of one which exploded about three miles off when the bell was on the bottom I felt it unwise to take any risk as they approached within a mile.

We have undoubtedly been very fortunate to escape disaster as those now found are quite close to us, the last being a few hundred feet off and how we could have missed them after all the dragging around in the area I do not know.

The demolition of C-deck continued. The steward's room was blown and torn apart. The *Niagara*'s silverware—serving trays, sugar bowls, milk jugs, knives and forks—now began to be hauled up in the grab. The crew kept pieces of it as souvenirs. The wall of the passageway between the steward's room and the bullion room was the next to be demolished and a door with a small porthole in it, identified as being just forward of the bullion room, was brought to the surface. (This door in on display at Kelly Tarlton's Shipwreck Museum at the Bay of Islands, New Zealand.)

The hole in the *Niagara* continued to widen. Johnstone continued to tear more cardboard from his model.

* * *

Between 13 June and 18 July the New Zealand Navy disposed of 71 mines in the area before considering it clear and declaring the minesweeping finished. Presumably many of the remaining mines sank, but for years afterwards a wayward German mine could still be found washed up on the beach somewhere around the Hauraki Gulf.

On 19 July, the minesweeping finished, the observation chamber was lowered carefully inside the hole blown in the *Niagara* until its bottom was resting on the wreck. On the surface a mark was made on the plaited rope suspending the chamber. Then it was slowly raised until John Johnstone reported the bottom of the chamber was level with the outer hull of the wreck. Another mark was made on the suspending rope. The distance between the two was measured and found to be 24 feet. This, according to the logbook, proved that: 'the bottom of the bell had landed on the bullion room'.

EIGHT

21 July – 13 October 1941

A Piece of Precision Machinery

Paragraph seven of the contract between the Commonwealth Bank of Australia and the United Salvage Syndicate states: 'Before removing any bullion the Commonwealth Bank of Australia needs to be notified by code. Removal can only occur when bank official has arrived.'

With the observation chamber having touched the bullion room, Williams now sent his coded message requesting that the bank send their official. Victor Neilley, a former head teller was called out of retirement and asked if he wanted to go to New Zealand to witness the recovery of the gold. He readily agreed.

While Neilley was travelling to New Zealand, Williams was having a frustrating time as minor mishaps plagued progress in clearing the area around the bullion room. The weather made work impossible for a number of days, then a mooring line gave way. When the mooring wire was brought on board it was found to have been cut cleanly through at a depth of 40 fathoms and a mine was suspected. Williams returned to Whangarei, picked up his spare mooring block and returned to sea.

By 31 July the new mooring block was layed in position and diving recommenced. The next day a curious entry appears in the logbook of the *Claymore*: 'At about 2 p.m. a large Japanese tramp steamer passed close under the stern of the salvage vessel having apparently altered course for that purpose'.

When fitting out the *Claymore* Williams had originally asked for naval protection. He was given two World War I .303 rifles and 100 rounds of ammunition. On a number of occasions the logbook records that an anchor light wasn't exhibited at night due to the 'suspected presence of raiders'. Whether they were being observed by the Japanese or not, Williams, Herd and the Johnstone brothers were all very aware of the growing hostility in the area.

'We had all spent enough time in the Pacific to know the meaning of 'face' to Asians and none of us believed that Japan would lose a great deal more of it before there was war in the Pacific,' James Herd later told a journalist.

* * *

Less perhaps has been written about the chain of events that led to war in the Pacific than has been written about the war in Europe. But still the subject has been recorded enough times for me to assume that only the briefest details will need to be given here.

It was a chain of events that began almost 90 years earlier. In 1853 Commodore Mathew Perry of the U.S. Navy sailed a squadron into Tokyo (then Yedo) Bay, ending Japan's isolation. Japan was forced into trading with the rest of the world and European powers soon followed the Americans in negotiating trading concessions with Japan. Recognising that only modernisation along Western lines would prevent their country being divided up among the 'great powers', and fuelled by intense national pride, Japanese society underwent a transformation. The Meiji Restoration (1868-1912) saw the end of feudalism, the introduction of a modern taxation system, the emergence of a centralised bureaucracy and the encouragement of industrialisation.

Japan developed an army modelled on that of Imperial Germany and a navy modelled on that of Britain. A series of political manoeuvres saw Japan fight a war against China in 1894, against Russia in 1904, annexe Korea in 1910, then become an ally of Britain against Germany in World War I. Largely as payment for the its role in World War I, Japan was allowed to take over former German possessions in the Pacific at the end of the war. Japan's increasing power then became a concern for Britain and America, these two countries sought to limit the spread of Japanese influence in Asia and the Pacific. They did this with the Washington Naval Treaty which limited the number of naval ships Japan was allowed to build.

Japan resigned from the League of Nations in 1933. A year later it refused to be bound by the limitations of the Washington Naval Treaty. Its armies, and its influence, began to spread in China. In 1936 it signed the Anti-Comintern Pact with Nazi Germany and the Tripartite Pact with Germany and Italy in 1940.

By 1940 the United States of America was still not officially involved in the war in Europe, but was edging toward a closer agreement and increased support of Britain. Economic pressure began to be applied to restrict the expansion of Japan. As Japan was totally dependant on imported raw materials (for example, 80 per cent of its oil came from America) such economic pressure would have a telling effect. Japan became more determined, putting more and more resources into its armed forces, particularly its Navy. War in the Pacific became inevitable when Great Britain and the United States imposed embargoes on the sale of raw materials to Japan, effectively trying to 'starve' Japan into reversing its plans for expansion. These embargoes were placed on 5 August 1941.

*   *   *

On 5 August the *Claymore* was anchored over the wreck of the *Niagara*, clearing debris away from around the entrance to the bullion room. This was done by first lowering the chamber so the diver could get a clear view of the room. The diver would then direct the lowering of the grab. Once a load of rubbish was caught in the grab it had to be dumped clear of the wreck. This was done by lifting both the chamber and the grab until they were above the wreck, then slacking the mooring lines so the *Claymore* would drift away. Once clear of the *Niagara* the rubbish would be dropped from the grab, the mooring lines pulled tight, then the chamber and grab brought back into position and lowered to the bullion room again. Williams later wrote: 'Always before letting the *Claymore* run I insisted the diver make sure he and the grab were high enough above the *Niagara*'s deck to prevent catching on a davit, or some funnel stay on the boat deck'.

Work continued clearing rubbish from around the bullion room and the next day Bill Johnstone was down in the chamber late in the afternoon, guiding the clearing of debris. Williams wrote:

A PIECE OF PRECISION MACHINERY

I had suggested to Bill that he come up, but he had the grab down and was hopeful of getting a girder out of the way that had proved troublesome all day. 'Give us a few more minutes, skipper' over the phone and in about ten minutes more 'I've got it . . . shift us over A-deck so I can drop the piece'.

'Make sure you're clear' the order. A wait while the diver looks around and then . . . 'All clear, let go the moorings' . . . and the *Claymore* surges forward.

This time, watching the bell and grab wires, usually about ten feet apart, to my horror I saw them begin to close on each other, a sure sign one was foul.

Below, the davits swung out from the *Niagara* a year earlier to lower the lifeboats now protruded like giant hooks from A-deck. The grab had not been raised high enough and the wire had snagged itself on one of them. The *Claymore* rolled and strained at its moorings. As it did so the chamber wire took a turn around the grab wire and both were hooked on the wreck.

Jim Kemp remembered the incident.

As we could only handle him up and down, completely vertically, the only method we could use to free him was to take the *Claymore* away on a long angle, outside the edge of the moorings and pull from there and go right round the full circle until we found the right direction to pull. We didn't think we'd ever see him again. Or the bell.

It was almost three hours before the chamber, with Bill Johnstone inside, freed itself. The grab remained snagged. In his monthly report to the bank Williams wrote:

'. . . and have never been so thankful in my life as I was to see it rising to the surface safely. The grab would not come clear so we bore the *Claymore* down as far as we dared and then waited while the swell caused her to rise and fall, thereby causing a sawing action on the bottom. After about another hour, by a great stroke of luck it came clear, bringing with it a mass of rope and wire and other junk in which it had been caught.

Although he knew it had been caught badly W. Johnstone showed not the slightest perturbations about it and told us calmly what was happening all the time. If he had lost his head he might have been there yet.

'He was just the same man that night', Jim Kemp recalled. 'Never even spoke about it. He was absolutely fearless, like his brother'.

The *Claymore* stayed over the wreck to continue work the next day. At 5.45 a.m. the logbook records a 'moderate gale and rising seas'. The *Claymore*'s anchor was secured to the head mooring and this suddenly parted. Before the side moorings could be slacked off, two lines had also parted and the *Claymore* swung around with her stern now facing into the waves. The sea broke over the stern and began flooding the ship. To turn it around so the bow faced into the storm, an attempt was made to pass a stern line to the bow. Mooring lines became tangled and one fouled the propeller.

The *Claymore* clung to one mooring line being dragged slowly along at the mercy of the gale. The kauri buoy that had parted from the head mooring block was tangled in the one mooring line that secured the *Claymore* and now thrashed around threatening to smash a hole in the hull.

Despite the gale Williams was anxious to recover the original mooring line that had parted. He was suspicious that the contractor who had made up the five ton concrete mooring blocks might have used inferior cement. If he could recover the line and show that the mooring block had broken up, he would be able to demand compensation from the contractor. The logbook reads:

An attempt was now made to lift the buoy on board, but when the vessel was alongside it became obvious that the man hooking it would be seriously hurt or that the buoy would fracture the shell plating [hull]. It was therefore decided to attempt to secure the buoy and tow it under the lee of the [Passage] Islands. The ship was therefore brought near and a bight [loop] of wire thrown over the log and a heavy shackle run down the bight thus securing the log by its mooring [line]. The wire was passed aft and the ship stopped until the propeller was clear.

The weather became steadily worse and although the ship was steaming full ahead slow progress was made and the decks were continuously flooded fore and aft. At 3 p.m. the lee [shelter] was gained under the middle Chicken [Island].

In the relative shelter of the Chicken Islands the kauri buoy was lifted on board and an attempt made to bring up the mooring line. The line became foul of something on the seabed and: 'although a strain heavy enough to lift ten times was brought to bear on the wire it could not be recovered'.

Williams pulled on his 'piece of evidence' until the stern of the *Claymore* began to bury itself under the water. But the wire would still not come free. Finally, in danger of flooding the *Claymore*, he gave the order and a crew member waded aft in the water swirling over the deck and hacked through the wire with an axe. Williams monthly report to the bank concluded: 'with this in mind I have knocked a piece off the spare block and am having it analysed so that we may know whether or not the contractor who made it has not skimped on the cement'.

* * *

When the *Claymore* returned to Whangarei it was greeted by the bank's representative, Victor Neilley. By all reports Neilley, a keen amateur fisherman, came to thoroughly enjoy his time aboard the *Claymore*. His first report to the bank stated:

The crew are all busy adjusting grabs, splicing ropes and wires, trimming the coal bunkers, which is work they can do in unfavourable weather. The whole proceedings are most interesting to me and Captain and crew have made me welcome in every way. During the meal times the conversations and yarns go near vulgarity, but the ordinary seaman has that privilege.

August saw another visitor on board the *Claymore*. After the New Zealand Navy had assisted him in obtaining guncotton, Williams had written a letter of thanks to the Secretary of the New Zealand Naval Board. The letter also said:

As far as I am aware the equipment in use on the job is the only gear of the kind in the Southern Hemisphere and, having in mind the possibility that the Board may at any time be faced with the necessity of deep diving, it has occurred to me that Members might like one of their Officers to see the nature of the work that is going forward, in which case I would be glad to welcome him.

The New Zealand Navy accepted Williams invitation and Lieutenant Haynes, RN (Rtd), spent a week on the *Claymore* and even went down in the observation chamber accompanied by John Johnstone on 18 August. His three-page report reiterates the details of the salvage and includes his personal observations:

Although outside the scope of this report the importance of the undertaking . . . is excuse for including in my remarks a brief description of the salvage party and the methods employed.

On my first acquaintance with the s.s. *Claymore* and her salvage crew the whole position struck me, to say the least of it, as ludicrous. An old ill-equipped vessel with a total complement of 15, ten only of whom are actually engaged on the wreck . . . many of them mere boys, were tackling the most difficult salvage job yet attempted. Unlike the salvage of the 'Egypt' they were working throughout winter in a greater depth of water and pestered by enemy mines. Up to the present the weather has permitted but 170 working hours of a total of 199 days since the *Niagara* was located.

It took me but a short time living and working with them to realise that contrary to my first impression the work is in the hands of two of the most able and efficient masters engaged in salvage undertakings, Captains J. P. Williams and James Herd, aided by divers John E. Johnstone whom I regard as one of the world's best divers, and Chief Shipwright W. Johnstone, on loan from the Royal Australian Navy. The divers are brothers.

The secret is leadership and teamwork. The whole team live together and under the leadership of Captain J. P. Williams function like a piece of precision machinery.

Publicly, Williams and his crew must have appeared to work together in a spirit of leadership and teamwork. Privately the stress of the work was beginning to show, even on the patient and loyal James Herd. In a letter to his wife he wrote:

. . . no one can say that this is a one man job and there will be a hell of a row, if when it is finished J.W. [Williams] takes all the credit. I know he will get the bulk of any cudos, but there are others to be considered. There are many things here of which I cannot write but I will tell you all about when next we meet. Anyhow whichever way things go after the job is through I will have the satisfaction of knowing that I did my part in bringing it to a successful conclusion but I suppose it will all be a seven day wonder and then be forgotten. Regarding the rewards promised by J.W., I will have to be at the mercy of the directors of the concern [United Salvage Syndicate], . . . this bunch will get the lion's share and we will get just what they think we should have, crumbs from the rich man's table.

Williams was driving himself to a point of illness. He suffered from stomach ulcers ('the result of eating the food they used to serve on the old sailing ships', I was told). As much as he pushed the men and coaxed them to work harder, he pushed himself more. By August he would confine himself to his cabin for long periods and Herd wrote: 'J.W. came out with us but he is a very sick man. I feel sorry for him, his colour is terrible and his cabin is nearly unbearable to go into, it has such a peculiar odour'.

While they all remained loyal to Williams, privately they expressed their concerns about the job. One concern obviously, was the fact that they considered they were being underpaid. The promise of bonuses went some way in alleviating that. Another concern was that Williams would get whatever 'glory' was coming if the job was successful.

To ensure secrecy, James Herd would burn his wife's letters after he had read them, but it appears (as so often was the case) that more was known in Australia about what was happening on the *Claymore*, than on the *Claymore* itself. On September 7th Herd responded to one of his wife's letters by writing: 'Was glad to have your news about Captain Hillington and the tripe he gave about J.W. writing a book. J.W. is not writing a book [about the salvage]'.

Williams was not himself writing a book about the salvage, but was, in fact, planning to have one written. One of the United Salvage Syndicate members, Donald Mackay, visited the Commonwealth Bank of Australia and a bank memorandum states:

Mr Mackay visited the bank re having a writer on board the *Claymore:*

Mr Mackay pointed out that this approach [referring to an approach by a New Zealand journalist] raised the question of the literary aspects of the salvage operation. He said that the salvage undertaking was probably the most difficult of its kind ever attempted and the experience obtained during the course of the operations would be of untold benefit in this field of salvage work. The story, apart from its scientific value, would have definite commercial value if properly presented.

I understand from his advice that neither Mr Mackay nor other members of the Syndicate were financially interested in the commercial presentation of the work and that any monetary gain would be for the benefit of Captain Williams and Chief Diver Johnstone, as any proper story eventually written could only come mainly from their logs, diaries and other material. In addition those men, together with their crew, have undertaken all the risks and hazards necessary in carrying out the work.

Donald Mackay then sought a writer to record the story and the bank recommended Ion Idriess. The books of Ion Idriess are well known and considered classics of Australian adventure, but Donald Mackay (according to a further bank memo) was:

... far from impressed with Mr Idriess's qualifications. He [Idriess] was not available to join the *Claymore*. Mr Idriess stated that he would be able to write the story from notes and did not attach much importance to the personal aspect.

Mackay went to Mr Warwick Fairfax of the Sydney Morning Herald who likes the idea. Has arranged for two men to join the *Claymore* as members of the crew.

Mr Fairfax's representatives will take notes and cinematograph films of the operation.

James Taylor, a veteran journalist with the *Sydney Morning Herald*, was given the assignment. He later wrote how he returned to his home on 24 September 1941 to find several urgent messages, all asking him to telephone his Chief. As it was late in the evening Taylor thought his response could wait until morning.

Naturally the Chief was not excessively amused when I presented myself bright and early. He was terse. He was curt. It was evident he did not approve of people who were not perpetually on call . . . he came to the point with a jerk.

Could I leave for New Zealand?

A PIECE OF PRECISION MACHINERY

I supposed so. Yes of course I could. When?

'You will go almost immediately', he went on, transfixing me with his eyes.

'I can't tell you what you will be doing there. The whole business is secret. Very'.

Taylor was joined by an American cinematographer, J. M Leonard, who was working in Australia at the time. The two of them left for New Zealand and joined the *Claymore* on 10 October.

*   *   *

While Taylor was being briefed by his chief, in New Zealand the *Claymore* crew were attempting to blow the door off the bullion room. With the *Niagara* over on its port side the door was now above the room. It was Williams intention to first try and blow the door 'clean off', so as not to damage the walls of the room. It was presumed the gold would now be resting against the far wall, which was not designed to hold such a weight. Blasting away at the upper wall could fracture the lower one and cause the gold to fall through. Williams' report to the bank stated:

After giving the matter a lot of thought it is my intention to try first to get the door off the room and grab what may be got through there before trying to shoot the corner off. With this in mind I have designed and ordered locally a very small grab for this particular job. It will not be ready for us this time so, if we manage to get the door removed I shall come in and wait for it. If on the other hand the door cannot be got clear, which is quite possible, then I shall proceed to shoot the top in the ordinary manner and trust to luck that the bottom of the room will hold.

While he was waiting for his small grab to be made, Williams proceeded to sea. The logbook, 24 September 1941 records:

At 11.00 a.m. the Chief Diver made an examination, and as the visibility was reasonably good, reported that he can clearly see the alleyway alongside the bullion room and had in fact, landed the stem of the bell therein.

After discussion it was determined to place a 3 inch—12 pound shot between the lock and the alleyway with the idea that it would (a) probably blow the door back on its hinges or (b) would shatter the rivets along the corner angle.

A very heavy swell was running all day causing the salvage ship to rise about 12 feet, thus making the placing of the shot a matter of difficulty.

Ultimately it was well placed, but unfortunately misfired.

... the stern mooring parted on the bottom, the ship surged forward, sweeping diver and shot some 60 feet across the bilge keel and work had to be abandoned for the day.

The next day the same thing was tried again. John Johnstone was able to place the shot successfully and after the chamber had been brought back on board the explosive was detonated. The crew now waited for the mud to settle, because visibility was almost nil after an explosion. Finally at 3 p.m. the chamber was lowered. Johnstone was able to report that the door had been blown clear off its hinges and had fallen inside the bullion room.

The *Claymore* returned to Whangarei to wait for the smaller grab to be completed.

Chief Engineer Jim Kemp had been experimenting with an underwater lamp, and this had now been constructed. It necessitated a generator being brought on board the *Claymore* to supply electricity. (A bonus to the crew because the generator could also provide electric lighting and refrigeration.) The next trip out (logbook, 1 October):

The diver took the new lamp down with him and confirmed that the door of the bullion room had been blown in, together with part of the frame. The lamp was lowered into the room but owing to the rise and fall of the salvage ship it kept bumping inside and thereby raising clouds of mud which totally obscured vision. After repeated attempts the light container was finally lowered inside and the distance from the door, until it came to rest, measured as being six feet. This would indicate that the contents were unmoved.

Next, hooks were tried in an attempt to tear open the bullion room. Watched by the diver in the observation chamber, these were lowered inside, hooked, then the strain on the holding wire taken up and the rising and falling of the *Claymore* would be used to pull at the walls. This practice was abandoned because the hooks would jerk free and crash into the nearby observation chamber. It was correctly supposed that if a hook hit a glass porthole the glass would shatter and the occupant would be immediately crushed.

After a successful day laying and detonating explosives on 6 October, a section of the bullion room wall was brought to the surface now leaving an opening measuring eight feet by four feet. The small grab was lowered inside, but 'failed to open without jigging, much to the danger of the diver'. It was decided to return to Whangarei to have the small grab modified.

The *Claymore* tied up at the Whangarei Town Wharf on 7 October. Waiting for it were author James Taylor and cinematographer J. M. Leonard, who had just arrived from Australia.

* * *

The same day in Australia the coalition government, under Arthur Fadden, resigned because it did not have the numbers to carry a motion in the Lower House. Fadden had come to power only six weeks earlier when growing dissension in the coalition had caused Robert Menzies to resign the leadership. When two independents withdrew their support the new government was forced to resign. John Curtin, the leader of the Labor Party, was commissioned as Prime Minister. Within a couple of months Curtin was proclaiming that Australia now 'looked to America for protection in the Pacific, free of its traditional ties to Great Britain'. I mention this here only because of the repercussions the change of government would have for Williams and his crew after the completion of the salvage.

* * *

Also on the same day, in a letter to the Commonwealth Bank, Williams again took the opportunity to complain about the lack of support from the New Zealand Navy:

Before leaving this time I telephoned to the Commander of the Naval Base at Auckland telling him of the position and suggesting that we should have an escort for a few days when the recovery of the gold began. His reply, Bingley of whom I have written before was the person involved, was to the effect that he could not see any reason why an escort should be necessary. It had occurred to me that outside of the possibility of interference from a raider, one would have thought it a good plan to have a vessel alongside this old craft in case she should founder with the spoils, but Bingley's mind apparently does not work that way and I do not, therefore, intend to do anything more about it.

In a letter to G. M. Shain, the bank's representative in Melbourne, Williams expressed his final doubts:

My mind seems unable to realise somehow that it will be recovered so soon and I find myself constantly trying to imagine some unforseen trouble such as the possibility that the boxes are jammed in like a solid mass by the swelling of the wood in the water, or that the room and its contents are lightly held that even the weight of the grab will cause it all to go and rob us at the last.

With Victor Neilley, James Taylor and J. M. Leonard now additional passengers, the *Claymore* sailed for the wreck on 11 October. Some of the mooring blocks had dragged out of position and the next day was spent putting them back in place. It was not until the afternoon of 13 October that John Johnstone could be lowered in the observation chamber to guide the small grab into the bullion room. James Taylor witnessed the lowering of the chamber for the first time:

The grab had now been swung over the side and Johnstone was being clamped into the bell, from which he was exchanging words with Captain Williams over the telephone. The diver was never lowered until the telephone had been properly tested. Too much depended on the efficient working of this instrument to take chances with it.

'O.K.', announced Johnstone at length. O.K. it was. The winch began to revolve, and slowly, cumbrously, the monster was lifted from its bed in the hold and over the side, the *Claymore* listing several degrees as she took the weight. The bell, I noticed with surprise, was almost buoyant when it submerged to the level of the top of its dome. There was practically no strain on the suspending wire until the diver filled his ballast tank.

A PIECE OF PRECISION MACHINERY

'Lower the grab', ordered the captain, following up his instruction a second later, with: 'Lower the bell'.

Matters were so contrived that the grab was seldom above, or too near, the bell. 'One of the first safety rules of diving', Bill Johnstone had told me, 'is not to have any weighty object over your head. For all you know it might crash and put your lights out for ever'.

Down went the grab. Down went the bell. Minutes passed and still the winch ends were steadily revolving, unwinding their respective wires at the rate of 60 feet a minute.

'Hold the bell—hold the grab'.

Captain Williams' tone was matter-of-fact, but his words were obeyed in an instant. The deck crew knew only too well there was no margin of latitude between an order and its execution. Even inches are vital in undersea work. A diver is never many inches from death.

John Johnstone described what he could see from the chamber:

The bell landed on the boat deck, a bird's eye view for me.

'Lowering the grab'.

'Lower away it is', I replied. 'Land it, then open and take a bite'.

Two big harpuka were sightseeing, attracted no doubt by the white paint. These fish were always around.

'Take it up and drop it again'.

I could hear the clang of metal against metal. I did not want to hear this. What I wanted to hear was a dull thud. The gold bars were in pine boxes.

'Up more skipper and drop quickly'.

This did it, for this time there was a dull thud.

'Open and take a bite'.

I heard the crash of timber as the teeth of the grab closed.

'Take it up steady'.

From the darkness emerged the closed grab. From my window I saw one box firmly held.

'Hold everything and take up the bell'.

'Anything wrong?' asked the skipper. 'What about the grab?'

'Just hold it where it is and get me up'.

Watching proceedings above James Taylor wrote:

After a thousand years Johnstone was standing on the bridge-deck whispering to his chief, whose gaze was riveted on the spot where the grab would ultimately break water.

'I think it is something worth while', I overheard the diver say. 'It looks like it but I won't swear to it. The teeth have a good hold. Anyway we'll soon know'.

All who could do so rushed to the rail, counting each foot of the grab wire as it wound in like a tired snail.

'There she comes', shouted Captain Herd. 'Steady it is'.

'Hold the grab'.

As it swung a few feet above the surface, spouting cascades of water, we saw that the spiked teeth had bitten into the corner of a mud caked box and were holding it firmly between the grab and the apron underneath.

'By the gods. It's gold. It's true. It's really true. I can't believe it . . . Johnstone is that gold?'

The Captain could hardly trust himself to speak. He was very pale.

'Not a doubt' the diver assured him.

Anyway we dropped the box onto the deck, and there was great excitement as you could imagine', Ray Nelson recalled. 'Everybody was yelling and cheering. So anyway we cleaned those off and Captain said, 'Well boys, down to the saloon'.

We had our solemn moments as well, because Captain Williams being an old English sailor had a big portrait of the King in the saloon. We drank the King's health, sang 'God Save the King' then proceeded with the celebrations.

Old Johnno sat at the head of the table with the two bars held in a V for victory sign. We got a photo of that. Yeah, that was a great day.

NINE

13 October – 10 December 1941

When a Prince He Rises with his Pearl

Gold!

No other metal has captivated man's imagination more or driven him to greater deeds of heroism or treachery. Gold lured the Egyptians to explore the African continent. It drove Cretans and Phoenicians to the edges of the then known world. When Christopher Columbus set foot in the 'new world' in 1492, the first thing he asked the natives was, 'Where's the gold?'

Gold made men think they were gods. It made them murderers. Gold justified the slaughter of civilisations and the ransacking of centuries of art treasures. For 6 000 years gold has had properties that have made it prized above all else. Its colour is one. The sheer lustre of its yellow attracts. The Pharoahs considered it the symbol of the sun's rays. The Incas called it the 'tears of the sun'.

Gold is durable and malleable. Jewellers can fashion it into intricate shapes of adornment. Even in ancient Egypt a skilful artisan could hammer gold into such fine leaves that it would take 250 000 of them to make a pile one inch high. Gold is ductile. That is, it has the ability to be mechanically deformed without cracking. One ounce of gold can be drawn into a wire so fine that it could stretch 50 miles.

Gold is dense. Specifically 19.32 times heavier than water. So dense that the 100 000 tons man has mined since 4 000 BC, if combined in one block, would be of a size no larger than a small suburban house.

And gold is almost chemically inert. It does not tarnish. It does not corrode. Today, if the gold bars that still remain inside or scattered around the wreck of the *Niagara* were brought to the surface, they would be as shiny as they were the day the ship hit the mine.

* * *

Without a radio, the *Claymore* had no means of contacting anyone to explain that gold had been recovered. As Williams and the crew celebrated in the saloon, the New Zealand Navy, the Commonwealth Bank and the people of Whangarei were unaware of their success.

On the same day, and in response to a letter from Williams a week earlier, the Commonwealth Bank of Australia cabled the Bank of New Zealand, asking for their support in the venture:

Salvage operation being conducted in New Zealand waters on our behalf is now approaching final stages. Goods are property of U.K. authorities. May we have your assistance in bringing the following before appropriate government authorities -
   (a) Naval protection to be provided while actual recovery is being made.
   (b) The need for strict censorship to ensure no publicity.

As regards (a) the amount involved is approximately 2 to 3 million pounds sterling thus the Empire's interest calls for all practical protection. Salvaging vessel is old and not particularly seaworthy.

The next day the *Claymore* crew resumed work over the wreck. Although they were able to grab all day without interruption, no gold was recovered. The following day (15 October) the *Claymore* was again brought into position above the *Niagara* and:

...the removal of further debris from the bullion room began. At 11.00 a.m. a box of gold was brought to the surface and safely taken aboard. At 11.40 another was recovered. On this occasion the box was gripped right at the end. The weight of the gold had caused the other end to fall out but the bars very fortunately were caught in the apron under the grab.

At 2 p.m. four boxes came up in the grab, three being full and one being empty. During this day nine boxes valued at approximately £72 000 were brought on board.

The *Claymore* now had twenty gold bars on board. Total weight over 8 000 ounces. Total value on 15 October 1941, when the

Commonwealth Bank of Australia was buying gold for £10 13s. 0d. per ounce, was £85 200. More than three times the current cost of the salvage to the bank.

Ashore, the recovery of the gold was still unknown. The attempt to get the *Claymore* a radio and some form of naval protection continued. On instruction from the Bank of New Zealand, the Director General of the Post Office now sent a cable to the Naval Secretary:

In view of the circumstances of the case and subject to your concurrence, it is proposed to accede to the request, and to supply a suitable installation [Radio] on loan for the period required, a ship's licence being issued to cover the operation thereof. The proposed conditions of operation are that the equipment is to be operated only in emergency and that all messages are to be coded. It is understood that a suitable code will be arranged between Captain Williams of the *Claymore* and the naval officer in Charge, Devonport Naval Base.

On 16 October the weather deteriorated and Williams decided return to Whangarei. At 11 a.m. the *Claymore* anchored in Urquharts Bay. Williams walked up the hill to the Manaia Gardens Guest House, where he could use the telephone. He rang the manager of the Whangarei branch of the Bank of New Zealand to say that he had recovered gold and was bringing it in. Williams returned to the *Claymore* and it now sailed up the harbour to the town.

'We had every flag of every kind—no matter what is was—everything was up, flying', Arthur Bryant recalled of that journey up the harbour.

'I don't know how the word got out, but about half the town was there to greet us', Ray Nelson remembered. 'Everyone was yelling and cheering'.

Slowly, but with a dignity and pride that one must imagine, the old *Claymore*, the ship that had been left to rust on the banks of Auckland Harbour, with its broken propeller and patched-up hull, with its crew of old men and young boys, with its bizarre looking observation chamber, with its maze of makeshift derricks, ropes and winches—and now with its prize of gold—steamed towards the wharf, where, from the crowd that had gathered, an enormous cheer erupted.

Only when the gold was safely delivered to the bank in Whangarei could Victor Neilley issue Williams with a receipt. Neilley then sent a telegram to the Commonwealth Bank of Australia, saying: 'Have today received from Captain Williams at Bank of New Zealand 20 bars of bullion contents of 10 boxes. Identification marks on all boxes obscured. Proceeding to Auckland next trip. Neilley.'

A flood of congratulatory telegrams came back.

In Whangarei, the day after the first gold was brought ashore, the crew were given a day off. The day after this however Williams was ready to sail again, but delayed departure while the Post and Telegraph Department fitted a radio to the *Claymore*. In the logbook he wrote: 'It's difficult to withhold the comment that the Naval Authorities should have steadfastly refused to allow us a wireless set until I brought in a substantial quantity of gold'.

The next trip out the *Claymore* anchored over the wreck for three days. On the first day the visibility was so poor that Johnstone could not see anything. The following day it cleared and four boxes, with eight bars of gold, were brought to the surface. Another eight bars were recovered on the third day, and the *Claymore* returned to Whangarei on 22 October.

Two day later it left for the wreck again, spending the following day sheltering from a storm at Passage Island. On Sunday the 26th the weather deteriorated. Commenting on the crew's belief that Sundays were unlucky, James Herd, in a letter to his wife, said: 'Do you know we have never been able to work on a Sunday? Most of the accidents occur on a Sunday. Today the weather is vile. Perhaps it will clear up and we can make another start tomorrow'.

The weather did clear for a few hours on Monday. Time enough for four boxes and one loose bar of gold to be brought up. Then the weather deteriorated again. Apparently it was a particularly rough storm for the logbook records: 'At one period the vessel 'pooped' badly whilst as she plunged forward a heavy sea flooded the fore deck, no damage resulted although on one occasion the whale boat stowed on the top rail of the foredeck was seen to be waterborne'.

Even Victor Neilley in a report to the bank felt compelled to write about the weather this trip:

... we hung on to the buoy from morning, hoping against hope and although we all expected a change the climax was not reached until 3 a.m., when the winches were set going to clear the moorings and make for home. And what a trip. What a night.

I think it was the immortal bard, in Macbeth or one of the Kings that said 'I have passed a terrible night, with awful dreams and terrible sights'. Well whatever he said or meant I'll double him.

The seas were coming over both ends. In fact one sea hit us amidships, came over the side and the water and spray was well over the top of the engine room. How the old ship stood up to it is a miracle to me.

* * *

Forty-five bars of gold had been recovered in three trips—18 000 ounces. But this was a mere trickle compared with what was about to come.

The *Claymore* steamed for the wreck on 31 October.

In the following three days 17, then 15, then 25 bars of gold were recovered.

Until November 4th, the bullion room door, which had been blown off its hinges, was lying on top of the gold and the recovery had been slow. Now, carefully guiding the grab, John Johnstone was able to watch it take a 'bite' at the corner of the door. Hanging precariously it was brought to the surface and taken on board the *Claymore*. Work was temporarily interrupted while the crew posed for photographs beside it. On the same day fourteen bars of gold were recovered. Then nine the next day.

But with the door out of the way, a clear working day meant that the grab could really scoop up the gold. 'It's like picking oranges the Johnstone brothers tell me', Victor Neilley wrote.

On 6 November, 66 bars were recovered.

After a week over the wreck the *Claymore* steamed back to Whangarei with 146 bars, over one and a half tons of gold on board.

It returned to the *Niagara* on 9 November and a record 92 bars were recovered in one day. A day later a further 36 bars were recovered, the *Claymore* returning to Whangarei with 51 200 ounces of gold.

Four more trips in November would bring the total gold recovered to 541 bars out of a consignment of 590.

'I must say', recalled Jim Kemp with a chuckle, 'that during the course of the recovery of the gold we all thought that we would be made wealthy men and maybe not have to work again. This was our great hope'.

The outstanding success of the salvage perhaps had the crew in a mild state of euphoria. To have so far recovered 541 bars of gold at a total cost equivalent to six of those bars perhaps led Williams, the Johnstones and the crew to believe that the Commonwealth Bank of Australia, with whom the contract was signed, or the Bank of England, to whom the gold belonged, would say something like 'What the heck, the salvage has exceeded everyone's wildest expectations, have something extra for yourselves. Maybe take a bar of gold each for the danger and hardship you went through. We've got plenty more thanks to you fellows'. But banks are banks and a deal's a deal.

Even Victor Neilley got caught up in the excitement of the success and wrote a letter to the Governor of the Commonwealth Bank asking if one bar of gold could be put aside, and medals struck from it to award to the crew. In his reply the Governor explained that he could not authorise the matter.

In fact in all dealings with Williams and the crew, the Commonwealth Bank continued to discharge its duties with the utmost propriety, following the original contract to the letter.

*   *   *

With the end of the job in sight the crew began planning a celebration to say farewell to the friends they had made in Whangarei. In a letter to Donald Mackay on 8 November, Williams wrote:

One thing I fear is that when the time comes the men will paint Whangarei redder than it has been yet, for they are straining at the leash now and planning all sorts of celebrations, amongst which one that would build a small float, hoist the Nazi flag on it, launch it from the Town Wharf here, then sink it with some of the leftover gelatine. I pointed out tactfully that this might easily send the *Claymore* to the bottom as well as blowing half of Whangarei up if they were not careful and the scheme is temporarily off, but it is an indication of the way in which their minds are working, and I am a little fearful of the outcome. I am fairly sure however that a plan to set up a bar for all and sundry has been already matured, and Whangarei will be treated to a sight of drunken sailors such as it has not yet had and it has had a little already.

Mrs Williams was also planning a ball but a telegram from the Governor of the Commonwealth Bank to Williams said: 'Understand you are contemplating a party on 9th December. In view of urgent need of secrecy we would much prefer that it should not be held.' The ball was cancelled.

Secrecy, as requested by the Commonwealth Bank at this point, was something of a farce. Six months earlier, after the thwarted attempts of Whatmore, Thomson and Davis to mount independent salvage efforts, Australian Naval Intelligence had pointed the finger at Gladys Williams as a possible source of information leakage. On 17 June they had cabled their New Zealand counterparts saying: 'The only matter which possibly calls for action is Mrs Williams talking. Will you please deal with her as you see fit.' The Intelligence Section of the New Zealand Navy replied that: 'Mrs Williams is being contacted by security regarding having talked too much'.

This contact, however doesn't seem to have done much good, because the Commonwealth Security Service continued to receive reports about friends of the Williams in Australia who were talking publicly about the most detailed aspects of the salvage.

Similar 'leaks' also originated from people in Whangarei. One person had written an account of the salvage and tried to sell it to New Zealand and Australian newspapers. The fact that both the New Zealand and Australian censors had already told the newspapers they were not to print anything stopped the story being published. Writing to Donald Mackay, Williams said: 'The fellow concerned is the accountant at the Whangarei Harbour Board, he lives just by the Railway Wharf and has thus been in a position to get the confidence of our people without them suspecting anything of his designs'.

The question now arose as to the point at which the salvage should be declared complete. That is, how long grabbing should go on for the remaining gold. Explaining his reasoning, Williams wrote to the Governor of the Commonwealth Bank on 29 November:

I have given a lot of consideration to the problem of whatever balance may remain as it will be somewhat difficult to know when to stop trying to recover them and possibly more difficult still for the Bank of England to realise why, since we have got so many we cannot get the lot.

In the first place some boxes have been lost from the grab and although we think this loss is restricted to three we do not know . . .

Secondly; although we think that the grab reaches all parts of the area in the long run there is no certainty that one or more boxes are not so placed as to make them impossible for the jaws to get hold of them, having in mind once more the angle of repose of the wreck . . .

Recently part of the internal structure of the bullion room came up in the grab and there was not a single rivet left in it, right to the bottom, from which it is obvious that the room must be hanging almost by the proverbial thread and that even a small shot will throw the lot to the bottom.

From this I have decided therefore after the last box has come up to continue grabbing until 200 unsuccessful bites have been made after which it would seem to me to be useless trying any more. There is of course the possibility that some may remain and should this be any substantial sum then I think we should consider sending Johnstone to America to enquire into the possibilities of helium gas for use with a flexible dress or whether the articulated suit would be of any assistance. This is however a point which can be thrashed out later, the present position being that we will, when the above has been followed, have exhausted the usefulness of our present appliances. It may be of course that all the boxes, saving those known to us have been lost, will be brought to the surface, but as far as I can see now this is unlikely and I want you to know what is proposed before hand.

* * *

At twenty minutes past two on the afternoon of Tuesday 2 December 1941, the *Claymore* left the Railway Wharf, Whangarei, and began the four-hour journey to the site of the *Niagara* wreck for the last time. It tied up to the north-east buoy and the crew waited out the night.

At five thirty the next morning they began mooring the *Claymore* in position. The weather was rough and when they lowered the grab they found it was bouncing dangerously, so it was decided to wait for the sea to flatten out. A second attempt was made in the afternoon and two boxes of gold recovered before the light failed.

On Thursday morning one box and two loose bars were brought up. Grabbing continued all afternoon. At one point the grab was inside the bullion room when the *Claymore* rose on a swell. The grab was trapped and couldn't rise with it. The resulting strain tore the hull block ring bolt out of one and a quarter inch steel plate. It was repaired and work continued, but as the logbook reports:

Despite the unfavourable conditions Mr Johnstone was able to raise 23 grab loads from the bullion room, in none of them was there anything but small pieces of concrete, broken spoons and other small items of table silver, but no gold. Since the last bar was recovered the grab has made 49 unsuccessful bites.

On Friday grabbing continued with no success. At 1.20 p.m. Williams went down in the chamber and was lowered inside the bullion room. The light was also lowered into the room. He wrote in the logbook:

At the time the water was clear and the bottom of the room could be very plainly seen and on it, apart from small pieces of concrete, there appeared to be nothing saving a fork, an empty bullion box, a few pieces of wood and other small debris. Later Captain Herd went down and confirmed the above. At 1420 Mr Johnstone managed to place the bell right in the room in such a position that every corner could be seen plainly. He reported it as having been cleaned right out.

On Saturday the logbook reports:

. . . bell overboard with Chief Diver and Master to examine debris for loose bars. Two sighted in all but possibility of recovery very doubtful indeed.

Fitted chisel teeth to grab and extended these four inches outside bucket. Diver in bullion room and for three hours attempted to dislodge two bars lying in the bottom of a foundation angle of D-deck. Ultimately one of these was knocked into the bullion room and recovered later.

At 1310 the Chief Diver took the light into the room consequent of the overhanging plate from the after end of the structure having been torn away by the grab thus leaving the whole area exposed. The light wire caught around the beam of C-deck and for some time the light could not be freed.

The grab was now fitted with spiked teeth—four each side and very shortly afterwards a box of gold and the bar from the foundation plate were brought to the surface.

Since the beginning of the salvage the crew had believed that Sundays were unlucky. If something was going to go wrong, it would go wrong on a Sunday. Equipment would fail, someone would be injured, a mine would be caught in the mooring lines—even the worst storms seemed to happen on Sundays.

Now the crew prepared for what would be their last Sunday over the wreck of the *Niagara*.

At 5.30 a.m. the *Claymore* was in position and Johnstone once again negotiated both the observation chamber and the underwater lamp into the bullion room. He reported that he could see every corner and that the room was clear. Williams then went down and reported the same thing. Then James Herd.

After breakfast Johnstone tried to manoeuvre the grab to pick up a loose bar that was lying in angle iron just outside the bullion room. This attempt was unsuccessful and, for the time being, the bar was left while Johnstone examined the area to see if he could find any other loose bars. Next Bill Johnstone went down in the chamber to also look for loose bars. He discovered a box among the wreckage on C-deck. There was one bar in the box and one bar outside it. Working for about two hours Bill was able to bump the bars to a place where they could be picked up.

In the afternoon John Johnstone went down again to attempt to get the bar just outside the bullion room. He managed to knock it back into the bullion room from where it could be picked up.

It was three-thirty in the afternoon. Total recovery was now 555 bars. Williams declared the salvage complete.

Crew members were now given the opportunity to take a trip down to the wreck in the observation chamber, accompanied by Bill Johnstone. Most of them jumped at the chance. Even the bank's representative, Victor Neilley made the trip to peer out a porthole at the sunken passenger liner.

At 7 p.m. the chamber was prepared for the last dive. The final passenger would be Tommy Nalder, the New Zealand able-seaman who had joined Williams in Auckland. Nalder and Bill Johnstone got into the chamber and it was swung over the side and began to descend.

From the outset the chamber's designer, David Isaacs, had repeatedly said that the ability of the glass to withstand the water pressure was an unknown factor. Now as the chamber reached 240 feet on its last dive, the glass in one of the portholes cracked from side to side. The chamber was brought quickly to the surface. Williams noted in the logbook:

That the bell should fracture on the last descent is no less extraordinary than the rest of the happenings today.

This is the first Sunday since the job began on which we have had any luck and on which some major or minor happening has not occurred to bring operations to a temporary halt.

It was Sunday 7 December.

New Zealand lies to the west of the international date line. As Williams was writing this logbook entry, in Hawaii, to the east, it was night-time on the previous day. The people there would wake to the Sunday that would 'live in infamy'. The Japanese attacks on Pearl Harbor and Singapore would bring war to the Pacific.

'When the bell was housed for the last time the crew cheered heartily though all of those declared they could not believe nor realise that the work was over.'

* * *

Perhaps out of tiredness, or relief that the job was over, Williams wrote no further entries in the logbook of the *Claymore*.

The *Claymore* stayed moored over the wreck for the night. The next morning the crew lifted their kauri logs from the sea and took them on board. A mine was found attached to one. No one could tell how long it had been there. The *Claymore*'s ensign was then dipped three times in a salute to the *Niagara*, Tommy Nalder played his piano accordion while the crew sang 'The Maori Farewell', then the *Claymore* returned to Whangarei. In his diary James Herd wrote:

Ensign lowered three times in salute to the old *Niagara* over which we have laboured all these months, amongst mines, bad weather and hosts of problems that are associated with a salvage job such as this. It is with mixed feelings that we leave this job now that the time has come for us to depart, we have had six days of ideal weather in which to complete the work. But we have achieved something and now look forward to returning to our homes. Noon. Full ahead for Whangarei, arrived 5 p.m. and learnt startling news of Japan having declared war on Great Britain and USA. Australia will now have a taste of war in reality.

Two days later the *Claymore* prepared to leave Whangarei. The Williams family, James Herd, the Johnstones and the crew all said their goodbyes. The tide to get the *Claymore* from the Town Wharf down to the mouth of the harbour was near to midnight, so the final departure was in the dark. On both sides of the river the people of Whangarei had parked their cars, pointing them downriver with their headlights on to make what Williams described as a 'golden pathway'. On board the *Claymore* Danny Scott, drunk from the celebrations, steered an erratic course. Tommy Nalder and Bluey Rigby played their piano accordions and the people on the ship and the people on the shore sang 'The Maori Farewell' to one another:

> Now is the hour when we must say goodbye,
> Soon you'll be sailing far across the sea . . .

As the *Claymore* disappeared from view the singing continued to be heard drifting over the water. In a sense, it still is heard in the hearts of the people I interviewed who were there that night.

TEN

25 December 1941 – The Present

Any Honour You Like to Name

News of the recovery of the gold had still not been made public. The Australian members of the crew arrived back in Sydney, then caught the train home to Melbourne, arriving on Christmas Day. As they celebrated their homecoming the Japanese were moving steadily south and Australia was reluctantly preparing itself for war.

On 10 January 1942 the Japanese minelaying submarine, I-124, accompanied by I-123, left Davao in the Philippines and sailed south in an attempt to sow minefields near the northern Australian port of Darwin. Ten days later I-124 was sighted and sunk with depth charges dropped by the Australian Navy Corvette, HMAS *Deloraine*.

I-124 came to rest in less than 150 feet of water. It was the first Japanese submarine of the war that, after sinking, was accessible to the Allies. Close to an Australian port and in relatively shallow water, it was hoped I-124 would be an intelligence goldmine. I-124 must have communicated with her naval base using the Japanese naval code, which it was generally thought at the time, had not been cracked. The Allies knew that Japanese Navy code books were equipped with heavy lead covers so they could be thrown overboard if a ship was in danger of being captured. In a submarine, however, they could not be so easily disposed of. If I-124 had settled on the bottom without major damage to its hull, then there was a good chance that a diver could get inside and recover the code books. American divers tried six days after the sinking, but owing to strong currents and poor visibility, were unable to get inside. The attempt was abandoned. It would not be possible until the neap tide slowed the strong currents in the Torres Strait. This would be in the second week in February. Expert salvors would be needed. Who better than the men who had recovered eight tons of gold from a ship 400 feet underwater?

Williams was given the job. Diving gear was loaded on the train in Melbourne and, accompanied by Arthur Bryant, taken to Darwin. Williams, John and Bill Johnstone, plus other Australian members of the *Claymore* crew, flew to Darwin.

Four days after they arrived Williams was having a salvage ship fitted out. While he was doing this Johnstone, Alf Warren and Arthur Bryant were 'on loan' to the Americans who were attempting to raise an oil barge that had sunk after a collision.

It was the morning of 19 February 1942. Johnstone was dressed in his standard diving dress and on the ladder of the diving vessel, about to get into the water. Alf Warren was adjusting his chest weights.

Arthur Bryant was assisting. He told me:

I heard aircraft and glanced up. There were about three wings of 30 in that first flight as I recall it and I looked across at the chap that I was working with and said, thinking that they were American planes, 'Look at that. Isn't that a fine sight. Now bring on your Japs'.

The next second I could have bitten my tongue off because after the planes, something blinked. That was a bomb as it dropped and turned and it blinked in the sun as it pivoted and then came hurtling down.

Just as the Japanese had completely surprised the Americans at Pearl Harbor, they now surprised the Australians at Darwin. Darwin was devastated. The possibility of going ahead with the salvage of the I-124 code books was abandoned. Williams ordered the crew back to Melbourne. They left a few days later when a train was available to take them south to Adelaide. Coincidentally, four days after the raid on Darwin, censorship on the *Niagara* salvage story was lifted. On Monday, 23 February, the *Sydney Morning Herald* ran the first of its 'scoops' written by James Taylor and photographed by J. M. Leonard. The headline read: 'Bullion From *Niagara*—Greatest Feat of Sea Salvage'. Arthur Bryant recalled:

I remember we were travelling on the train to Adelaide. We stopped somewhere and I bought all the newspapers. On the front pages were stories about the bombing of Darwin and the salvage of the *Niagara's* gold. We were travelling in a carriage without lights and I read the stories to the others by torchlight. We were all pretty excited. It's not often you make news in two separate stories that make the front page of the newspapers on the same day.

The *Niagara* story was very popular. T*he Sydney Morning Herald* and the other papers in the Fairfax group serialised it over five editions. The good news was tonic to a nation that was reeling from the blow of having just been bombed for the first time in its history. T*he Bulletin* wrote:

The story of the recovery of the *Niagara* gold reveals the gold of our own racial character as vividly did the bombing of England, the fight of the *Jervis Bay* and the defence of Tobruk. How can a British Commonwealth rich in such gallant and resourceful spirits be conquered?

*   *   *

But while the press was praising the 'courage, skill and enterprise' of Williams and his crew, there were members of the public service who were less impressed. L. J. Hartnett (later Sir Lawrence) wrote to the Minister for Munitions a week after Williams returned to Australia. In part the letter read: 'I feel it is imperative and my duty to bring to your notice what, in my opinion, is one of the most remarkable pages of history in Australia and accomplishment in this War'. Then after giving details, Hartnett went on to say:

Captain Williams has now returned to Australia after leading this remarkable expedition and knowing him personally, he is inclined to just consider the job well done and leave it at that. I know that it is causing him great concern that members of his crew, who performed such remarkable acts of gallantry have not received some official recognition.

. . . may I ask you to pass this on to the Prime Minister.

The letter was passed on to the Acting Prime Minister (R. M. Forde). The Prime Minister's Secretary then sent a memorandum to the Secretary, Department of Commerce. After setting out the basic details the memorandum said:

It would probably be found inappropriate for the same awards—either money or medals—to be given to all members of the crew: for instance, some would doubtless be more eligible for recognition for bravery than others.

In order to assist the Prime Minister in reaching a decision, it would be appreciated if you would be so good as to arrange for the following information to be supplied regarding captain and crew -

- Full names, addresses, ages, ranks, rates of pay and amount of any gratuitous payments they may have received;
- Nature of duties performed by each and length of service with the United Stevedoring Company;
- Suggestions regarding nature of the reward which might be granted each, i.e. plate, watch, money, decoration or medal; and
- Any further information which would be useful to the Prime Minister in considering the matter.

I should like to point out at this stage that this memorandum does not ask whether the Secretary, Department of Commerce, actually thinks some sort of award should be given or not. The idea that awards will be given is implied. The memorandum simply asks for information to assist the Prime Minister in reaching a decision as to what type of award should be given.

The paper trail that I am asking the reader to follow (for reasons that will soon be apparent) then leads to John K. Davis (no relation to the Davis's—uncle and nephew—involved in the 'alternate' salvage attempt). John Davis was the Director of Navigation, Department of Commerce (Marine Branch). The memorandum arrived on his desk and his reply needs to be quoted in full:

1. I agree with the statement made in Mr Hartnett's letter that this undertaking was a most remarkable and successful one carried out with skill and initiative, which have seldom, if ever, been equalled.
2. My personal views on the matter were expressed in a letter (herein) which I wrote to Captain Williams shortly after his return.
3. All this not withstanding, the question which must be asked is—Is the present an appropriate time for its official recognition seeing that the venture was primarily a commercial undertaking?

4. The British and Commonwealth Governments do make awards of money, plate, etc. but these are usually granted for gallantry in saving life at sea or for other deeds of individual heroism by seamen, such as saving a ship from destruction.
5. New Zealand minesweepers, in the ordinary course of their duty, were employed at the same time in minesweeping in the locality where the '*Niagara*' sank, and one minesweeper when so engaged was blown up with the loss of four lives.
6. The leader and members of the salvage party ought to be rewarded by those who have profited by their labours, as those concerned will no doubt derive considerable profit from the enterprise itself and the sale of various rights associated with it.
7. There is, as far as I know, no appropriate medal which could be issued to the members of the party for their part in this undertaking, nor am I aware of any recognition having been made by a Government authority in any other part of the world under similar circumstances.
8. The information asked for in (1) and (2) of the concluding paragraph of the memorandum from the Secretary, Prime Minister's Department, is being obtained and will be furnished as soon as available.

I will examine this reply paragraph by paragraph:
— With Paragraph 1, I agree.
— Paragraph 2 seems to imply that the letter from Davis to Williams is a reward in itself, or at least in some way compensation for what Davis is about to say in the following paragraphs. This letter from Davis to Williams is 208 words long and contains the following congratulatory message:

I could not help being reminded, as you told us of the almost incredible story of your recovery of the *Niagara*'s gold, of some lines from Paracelsus that were frequently quoted by Shackleton about two points in the adventure of the diver which seemed to me to have particular application in your recent undertaking.

One — when, a beggar, he prepares to plunge.
One — when, a prince, he rises with his pearl.

— Paragraph 3. Davis was asked for information. Not his opinion as to whether he considered it 'an appropriate time' or not. Having taken the liberty of suggesting it wasn't an appropriate time (for reasons he doesn't explain) he doesn't go on to say when would be.

– Paragraph 4 seems to imply that the actions of the men were somehow not in the right category for recognition, although I must admit the logic of the argument escapes me.

– Paragraph 5. Actually it was five lives. And Davis' logic seems to imply the crew of the *Claymore* would have been more eligible for some sort of recognition if they had succeeded in getting themselves killed.

– Paragraph 6. There was no 'considerable profit'. Not for the salvage syndicate, not for Williams. And certainly not for any member of his crew. Even if there were, would it be relevant in the recognition of gallantry? I think not.

– Paragraph 7. This paragraph simply reveals Davis' ignorance of the matter. When a British naval salvage party recovered gold from the *Laurentic* (in 120 feet of water, in peace time) the Commander of the salvage party was promoted and 11 Navy divers awarded the Order of the British Empire. A British Navy salvage party raised a German submarine off the Irish coast after the World War I and the commander was awarded the Distinguished Service Cross.

Mussolini himself pinned medals on the crew who salvaged the *Egypt's* gold.

– Paragraph 8. In this paragraph Davis promises to do the one thing he was asked to do. That is, supply the information so that the Prime Minister could make a decision.

The Assistant Secretary, Department of Commerce (Marine Branch) forwarded the Davis memorandum on to the Prime Minister's Department, adding his own observation (which also, was never requested):

Without in any way belittling the value of the salvage and the skill and enterprise shown and the dangers encountered in working at such depths, I feel that all those factors have been taken into account in the rewards received. When the War is over the Government will be in a better position to compare the services of these men with others rendered during the conflict and I suggest that no action in the matter should be taken until then.

No explanation is given as to why not—not even justification as to what right they had to give such an opinion. But the Prime Minister was happy to adopt this stance.

Even the Bank of England asked the Australian High Commissioner in London to approach the Prime Minister. The response was negative. The Bank of England advised the Commonwealth Bank of Australia: 'High Commissioner now advised by your Prime Minister that he considers nature of operation does not warrant special recognition beyond monetary reward already received'.

Williams persisted in writing letters, setting out the details of the salvage and praising the courage of James Herd, the Johnstone brothers and the rest of the crew, but to no avail. It was no secret that John Williams and the Labor government of John Curtin were not on the best of terms. Especially as Williams had a stevedoring business, and was seen as an employer in an age when the labour movement still considered that 'all bosses are bastards'.

James Herd wrote a letter to the Prime Minister, sending him press clippings regarding the salvage. As was the normal practice a draft reply was prepared for approval. The draft reply read:

Dear Captain Herd,

Thank you for your letter of 28th February and for the sentiments which you expressed.

I can assure you that I have taken a very keen interest in the progress of the salvage operations necessary to recover the gold bullion from RMS *Niagara* and can appreciate the great difficulties and dangers involved in these operations which rank as the greatest in salvage history.

I take great pleasure in congratulating you and your associates on the success of this work.

A note in the margin of this draft reply says: 'Dr Coombes says not to congratulate Capt. Herd as he was not in charge of the operations'.

At this point I now quote the Prime Minister's actual response to James Herd in full. I do this, at the risk of being repetitious but, to this day, the following letter is the only official recognition, award or acknowledgment any member of the crew of the *Claymore*, has ever received.

17th March 1942
Dear Sir,

I desire to thank you for your letter of 28th February, 1942 in regard to the salvage of the bullion from RMS 'Niagara'.

I am most appreciative of the great difficulties involved in the operations and it is gratifying to know that Australians were associated with such a magnificent achievement.

Yours faithfully,
John Curtin,
Prime Minister.

Before leaving the matter it is necessary, from the historical point of view, to say a little about John King Davis, the Commonwealth Director of Navigation who wrote the memorandum that apparently ensured that no honours would ever be given to the *Claymore* crew.

Born in England in 1884, Davis served on sailing ships before being appointed chief officer of the steam yacht *Nimrod* in 1908. The *Nimrod* took Ernest Shackleton's expedition to the Antarctic (during which time Shackleton trudged to within 97 miles of the South Pole). In 1909 it was Davis, now as master of the *Nimrod*, who took the celebrated group back to England. Two years later he was master of the *Aurora* and second in command of Douglas Mawson's Australasian Antarctic Expedition. He successfully completed many difficult voyages south, including breaking through the Ross Sea in 1916-17 to rescue the shore party of Shackleton's failed trans-Antarctic expedition.

He was appointed Commonwealth Director of Navigation in 1920, a position which he held until his retirement in 1949 (except for two years when he again went south with [now Sir] Douglas Mawson on the *Discovery*.

The Davis Sea, west of the Shackleton Ice Shelf bears his name, as does one of Australia's three Antarctic bases (the other two being Mawson and Casey). Davis died in Melbourne in 1967.

I was unable to learn why he felt so strongly about Williams and his crew not getting recognition for their work, although Jim Kemp did tell me that Williams and Davis had had a falling out before the War. 'Something to do with shipping in Melbourne'.

*   *   *

At this point it is also necessary to briefly summarise the costs and rewards associated with the salvage. Firstly, the value of the gold salvaged was £2 388 953. Thus the syndicate received, as its 2.5 per cent reward, £59 723 16s. 0d. From this it had to deduct approximately £10 000 for the manufacture of the observation chamber and other equipment. The wages and expenses of the salvage paid by the Bank of England to the syndicate amounted to approximately £25 000.

At the completion of the salvage the syndicate submitted a statement of expenditure requesting an additional £10 583 4s. 6d. for 'balance of wages, including special wages and overtime'. This amount covered the bonuses promised the men and the £3 000 bonus for John Johnstone. It brought the total cost of the salvage (exclusive of the 2.5 per cent reward) to approximately £35 000. The Commonwealth Bank of Australia replied that it was unable to authorise the payment, but would refer the matter to the Bank of England. This it did, saying in conclusion: 'in view of the very successful outcome of the operation we submit the Syndicate's application for your consideration'.

The Bank of England replied:

We have re-examined original contract and it appears, with the exception of some expenses not yet claimed, we have discharged our contractual liability.

Although I am reluctant to appear niggardly I should find it difficult to recommend payment over and above contract.

At this point (17 February 1942) the syndicate paid the bonuses to the crew out of its 2.5% reward. The Commonwealth Bank then got legal advice from the Crown Solicitor and further advised the Bank of England:

> He [the Commonwealth Crown Solicitor] has now advised me that in his opinion the claim of the Syndicate is probably chargeable against the expenses of the operation. Moreover he states that in his opinion a court would likely to hold the charges reasonable in respect of the contract and *award a reasonable amount in comparison with the costs of other dangerous salvage ventures.* [emphasis added]
> In view of this you may decide to meet the claim.

The Bank of England agreed to pay the bonus to the crewmen, but not the £3 000 for Johnstone.

This raised the question of taxation. Service personnel at the time were not taxed and the Governor of the Commonwealth Bank wrote to the Secretary of the Treasury, saying:

> The present incidence of Commonwealth Taxation, however, is such that a large proportion (in some cases by far the major proportion) of these bonuses will be lost to the men concerned, i.e. there will be the somewhat incongruous position that the bonus paid to the men by the British authorities for special national services rendered will in fact largely go to the Commonwealth Government in the way of taxation.
> It would appear that the nature of the highly successful work in which the men were engaged bears a national aspect, and we are writing you in the object of ascertaining whether the Government would feel disposed to place the captain and all Australian members of the crew engaged in this work, on the same footing as regards taxation, as members of the Australian Military Forces serving abroad.
> You will doubtless agree that there are special considerations warranting such a course, and I feel that it would be equitable to extend this benefit to these men.

In the end Prime Minister Curtin declared the wages and bonuses for the crew would be tax free. After the war, this 'tax free' declaration was again disputed.

Had the crew of the *Claymore*, at the completion of the salvage, united and put in a claim for salvage under the parliamentary act mentioned in Chapter 7, there is a possibility that they could have claimed an amount that, today, would be the equivalent of many millions of dollars.

Ray Nelson told me, 'We were all one crew on the ship. But after the job we went our separate ways and no one thought of putting in a salvage claim'.

It was only after the War that Jim Kemp, the Chief Engineer that joined the crew in April 1941, decided to do this.

* * *

After they got out of Darwin most of the Australian members of the crew worked for the newly formed Commonwealth Salvage Board, of which Williams was appointed chairman. They worked for the remainder of the war salvaging ships throughout the Pacific.

The salvage of the gold from the *Niagara* soon slipped from memory, and when mention of it did appear, it was often inaccurate. A French book of 1954 (*Underwater Exploration* by Philippe Diole) credited the whole job to Americans. *The Times Atlas of World War II* (in an obvious typographical error) calls the wrecked vessel the *Aliagara*. As recently as 1991 'one of New Zealand's foremost maritime historians' managed to get most of the details wrong including the name of the *Claymore* which is given as the 'Clansman'.

* * *

At the completion of the salvage the *Claymore* hadn't finished making a name for itself. It was returned to the New Zealand government, which planned to use it in the defence of Auckland Harbour. The *Claymore* was to become a Boom Gate Vessel (BGV), that is, one of the ships moored across the entrance to the harbour to keep intruders out. Hulks with a strong hull are usually used for the purpose. When considering the *Claymore* for this passive service it was noted that it 'must be in relatively good condition to have stood up to the strenuous salvage work on the SS *Niagara* in exposed waters under severe conditions'.

As a consequence it was estimated that the conversion would neither be very long nor particularly expensive. Two years later the New Zealand Navy's Chief Constructor was explaining to the

Minister of War Expenditure, why the job was still not complete and was estimated, so far, to have cost £29 000, earning the *Claymore* the reputation of being the 'most expensive Boom Gate Vessel afloat'.

* * *

Prime Minister John Curtin died on 5 July 1945. A week later Ben Chifley became Prime Minister. The matter of the taxation of the crew again came into question. Williams later wrote:

At Chifley's invitation I called on him at his office in Melbourne. On getting in I heard . . . 'What do you want? The thing was a waste of time, the gold is no use to anyone in New Zealand'. From me, 'If that is so why are you paying me ten pounds an ounce for the gold I'm producing at the Glenfine South Mine?' A grunt followed by, 'The workers money will be tax free. You are an employer and a capitalist, and anything you get will be taxed as unearned increment'.

I couldn't understand it, having toiled with our gang from first to last.

Williams and Chifley reputedly exchanged heated words before Williams stormed out. He took legal advice on the matter and found that, if he paid tax in New Zealand, he would not have to pay it again in Australia. This he did.

* * *

Johnstone and Williams had a handshake agreement that they would pool whatever money they earned (over and above their wages) and split it 50/50. Williams had made this offer after he had asked Johnstone to accept a reduced bonus of £3 000. In the end, as a result of only having a one-tenth share in the United Salvage Syndicate, and this money being taxed, Williams actually earned less from the job than Johnstone and the two men agreed to forget their arrangement.

* * *

Immediately after the war John Johnstone began planning his return to the *Niagara*, in an attempt to get the remaining gold. Williams argued that he had no right to do so. Their disagreement was so strong that, from 1946, until Johnstone's death in 1976, despite living in the same city, the two men were never to speak to one another again.

In one of his unpublished books Johnstone wrote:

It wasn't until after the war that I became 'freelance' and could come and go as I pleased. Work piled up to keep me going for years to come. New Guinea waters were cluttered with Japanese wrecks, then again there was the *Niagara*. I had never let up the idea of making another attempt to recover the 35 bars of gold that had been left behind.

Johnstone believed that the remaining gold could be recovered with an improved grab. The grab that had been used on the *Claymore* in 1941 was a large square type of two halves that came together, like that used for scooping up coal. It had worked while there had been piles of gold in the bullion room, but now there were only scattered bars and they would need to be plucked out of corners. A pointed grab would be needed. Johnstone wrote:

I had experimented in my workshop at home, making small lead ingots and studying how a grab should be shaped so that the lips of the two sides would draw together without lifting and grip the smallest object. I believed I knew how this could be done. The *Niagara* presented another problem that I tried to solve, the slope of her decks as she lay almost on her side. I was pretty sure that most of the gold remaining in her strong-room was on the higher side and hadn't been gathered up because the grab would always slide down to the lower part before it was closed. The answer to this had to be a smaller grab, or one that would lie where it landed. I worked long hours on these problems.

Johnstone tried to interest investors in backing his attempt to return to the *Niagara*. He sketched an idea for a diving chamber, like that used in 1941, but with an arm protruding from it. The arm had a mechanical claw on the end of it, which the diver inside the chamber could manipulate to pick up bars.

Returning to New Zealand in 1947, Johnstone attempted to get local investors, but was not successful. Then he went to England. He spoke to the Bank of England, saying he wanted to get the remaining gold and asked if he could have the 'rights' to salvage it. This must have presented a moral dilemma for the bank, which was fully aware of the remarkable work that Williams had done. The

Governor of the Bank of England wrote to his counterpart at the Commonwealth Bank of Australia asking for an opinion. In part the response said: 'There is no doubt in my mind that the success of the original expedition was entirely due to the combination of Captain Williams and J. E. Johnstone, neither of whom in my opinion, would have been successful without the other'.

Johnstone was given the 'rights' to salvage the gold. The agreement with the Bank of England was that the salvors would get 50 per cent of the value of any gold recovered.

Johnstone now told his ideas to the British Risdon-Beazley salvage group, which ran a professional salvage company with three fully equipped ships. They listened to Johnstone and told him they would consider his ideas. Johnstone returned to Australia and waited. It wasn't until 1952 that he got a reply.

Risdon-Beazley would be sending their salvage ship *Foremost 17* to Australia in the New Year and if Johnstone would act as an adviser they would attempt to get the gold from the *Niagara*. The *Foremost 17* sailed to Australia and at the beginning of 1953 salvaged lead and copper from the *Cumberland* in approximately 300 feet of water off the coast of New South Wales. After this job was complete it sailed for New Zealand, where Johnstone met the ship and its company at Auckland.

At this time Johnstone was almost 60 years old. He would not, as he was twelve years earlier, be the chief diver, but simply an adviser. He would help the team locate the *Niagara*, then use his knowledge of the ship to guide them to the bullion room. The *Foremost 17* had three ex-Navy divers. The chief diver was Harold Chadwick, the others were Dick Young and Frank Higgins. To reach the *Niagara* they had both an observation chamber like the one used in 1941 and an 'iron man' or armoured diving suit. This would be the first time such a diving suit was used in the Southern Hemisphere.

The *Foremost 17* left Auckland on 2 May 1953, to steam to the location of the *Niagara*. As a salvage ship it was clean, uncluttered, well equipped and sound ... everything the *Claymore* was not. It is perhaps ironic that as it pulled away from the wharf, less than 200 yards away, the old *Claymore* itself was finally being cut up for scrap.

Once the *Niagara* was located and the *Foremost 17* anchored over it Johnstone prepared himself to return to the ship he had known so well. He wrote:

How would I find things below? Would the wreck be as we had left it? Had the upper steel decks collapsed burying the gold bars? Then again the giant bull kelp and the prolific growth over the years could have engulfed the wreck.

The bell [observation chamber] was much the same as we had used but smaller and less cumbersome. I felt quite at home—a little excited maybe. I could hear Frank and Dick bolting down the lid. On my phone was the skipper. 'Lower me down 300 feet then hold the bell'. We could not have chosen a better morning for the visibility was 100%. Fish excitedly swam around. I was used to this. Soon the depths would beat them, and like as if an order had been given, they'd turn about and make upwards.

'You are now at 300 feet and I'm holding the bell' called Chads. I gazed through the ports but all was green haze. 'Lower another 30 feet or so'.

I first saw the muzzle of the 5 inch gun on the stern. Beyond that what appeared to be a submarine forest. It was just that. The giant kelp and marine growth had about engulfed the wreck. The aft mast stuck out, and the guy wires and rigging festooned with countless spiny sea urchins.

Johnstone recognised where he was and that he would need to be moved about 300 feet to be over the opening into the bullion room. But the deck railings and deck cabins could no longer be seen. Instead there was a forest of kelp that covered everything. After two hours of fruitless searching for the opening, Johnstone was brought to the surface.

For the next few days Johnstone waited while the younger divers cleared away the kelp forest with a combination of explosives and the grab. When they did eventually clear it away they found that the opening to the bullion room was now covered with the upper, 'A' deck which had collapsed. In the weeks that followed the crew continued to clear a way into the room. In fact, despite knowing exactly where the *Niagara* was, it still took the crew of the *Foremost 17* two months before they could actually lower their observation chamber into the open bullion room.

During that time they had tried using the 'iron man' suit that they had brought with them from England, but without success. At such depths the pressure of the water was so great that the diver found it impossible to move the arms or legs. The suit in fact became no more than an observation chamber—and a dangerous one because the protruding arms risked being caught when the diver was lowered inside the wreckage.

Now the job of trying to find one of the remaining 35 bars of gold began. The special pointed grab was lowered into the bullion room and raised over and over. But each time it only brought up mud and the silverware that had been stored in the steward's room. More weeks went by and the cost of the salvage was getting higher. The crew, and particularly the representatives of the English salvage firm, grew more cynical. They began to doubt Johnstone's judgment and he felt they thought the whole thing a hoax.

Then one bar of gold was brought to the surface. Perhaps it was down there after all. Enthusiasm returned to the salvage crew and over the next few weeks 29 more bars were recovered. 12 000 ounces of gold. Of the original consignment of 590 bars of gold, 585 had been recovered. Johnstone returned to Australia and the *Foremost 17* returned to England.

Five bars of gold remain lost on the *Niagara* to this day.

*   *   *

'On one of my business trips to London I was walking down Threadneedle Street', Chief Engineer Jim Kemp told me when I interviewed him in 1992.

And I passed this big four or five story building with only one entrance—no windows, no sign of any other opening. And at this door there was this big commissionaire who was looking very officious and I stopped and asked him what was the name of the building. He looked at me as though to say 'you little boy, you'.

'Listen son', he said. 'This is the Bank of England'.

So I said to myself 'by gee that's where I'll find out if there are any more bonuses coming'. And the next day I made it my business to go there. And after much difficulty, after being interviewed, almost fingerprinted, I finally got to see somebody. They first of all declared everyone was dead. And this wasn't long after the war. About 1955. Any rate, I once again told them I wasn't there to make any claims and that I wanted information and that I felt I could get what I wanted if they introduced me to the man with the files on the *Niagara*. This they did and they steered me up to a room on about the third or fourth floor. Any rate I was ushered into this office and they kept a close eye on me. Although I'd found by this time that if you didn't make a noise, didn't object and didn't go away, they didn't know how to handle you.

So he opened the files and he asked me some questions and we eventually got round to the part about the bonus. And he said we had been adequately reimbursed for our services.

Then later on [back in Australia] as I got to know more about salvage rights I mentioned this to my sister, who through her occupation with a leading solicitor in Sydney was able to get a legal opinion from Sir Garfield Barwick. Captain Williams was very interested in it and full of hope we would have done some good. We engaged Barwick on a percentage basis for the whole of the crew. After I'd written reams and reams of notes on the whole job he declared that we did have salvage rights, but we had lost them through the passage of time, the Statute of Limitations. So that was it.

*   *   *

Today little remains of the greatest gold salvage in history. Anyone wishing to see some remnant has few opportunities. The observation chamber is in the Market Museum, Castlemaine. Bits of silver plate from the steward's room brought up by the grab are in various private collections. The Australian National Maritime Museum in Sydney, has the piece presented by Williams to David Isaacs, the designer of the observation chamber, although on my last visit it was not on display.

In New Zealand the Wellington Maritime Museum has an excellent model of the *Niagara*. Kelly Tarlton's Shipwreck Museum 'Tui', at the Bay of Islands, has some pieces of silverware brought up in the grab along with a small door recovered from the hallway just forward of the bullion room.

Most other evidence is on paper.

There are, of course, the wonderful people I interviewed and to whom I owe a great debt of gratitude. But each is ageing, and from my conversations with them, pleased now to be left alone, to enjoy their families, friends and memories in their latter years.

Afterword

Les Mischewski was the youngest member of the *Claymore* crew. He'd gone to the barber's for a haircut and became part of history. After the completion of the salvage he never met any Australian member of the crew again. I met Les on my first trip to Whangarei. The fresh young face that beamed out from the photograph in the saloon the day the first gold was recovered now carried the lines and tarnish of a lifetime at sea, alcohol and cigarettes.

Les was living in a rented room in a boarding house. We brought in the camera, set up our lights and Les wheezed his way bravely through the video interview for almost an hour. Because we were recording sound as well we had to stop periodically while a train went past.

During the four years I researched and worked on the story of the recovery of the gold from the RMS *Niagara* I was moved by the simple dignity, courage and selflessness of many people. None more than Les Mischewski.

At the end of the interview I could think of no more questions. Les had answered everything and even sung a song he remembered the crew would sing while they waited for their dinner.

I started to signal the camera operator to stop rolling the tape, but paused. Les was about to say something. He looked down and spoke not to me and not to the camera. Not to anyone I imagine.

Well I can see them, but as they were, you know, different parts and different times on the ship where you run into them and you think of say, Danny Scott, you think of . . . you think of him on a certain part of the ship at a certain time. Captain Williams for instance. You remember him as he was sitting there talking to the diver. Johnno getting out of the bell. Bill getting into the bell. Things like that. But you never . . . your mind goes back all the time, but you never forget them. You think of them quite often. Through a year you'll often go back there. Just comes to you and you think of them all. They're tied up and you see them the odd night staggering back to the ship or something. That comes back to you, you know, things like that. My first call in the milk bar next to the Plaza Theatre there and having a milkshake. Something like that, but you never see them all again together, but they're always in your mind, eh, that's all. That's all I can say'.

Later on I decided this was an ideal way to end the television documentary. As Les was speaking I dissolved slowly to images of the people to whom he was referring, then back to him for the final shot. From there the screen goes to black, then the words appear:

This documentary is dedicated to the men, who during World War II, served aboard Salvage Vessel Claymore.

Then the end credits roll and the music comes up.

* * *

John Protheroe Williams continued to work hard all his life. He prospered and today the businesses he commenced are run by his family. For many years he served as Chairman of the Australian National (Shipping) Line. He was knighted for his services to Australian shipping. Captain Sir John Williams died in 1989 at the age of 93.

* * *

John Johnstone had the film he shot during 1941 edited and spent many years showing it at schools, clubs and anywhere that people were interested. Among his papers I found a letter of appreciation for showing it at the New York Explorer's Club. The film itself is silent and Johnstone would stand out the front and give the commentary live. By the 1960s he'd stopped showing it or giving talks on the *Niagara* salvage. By 1970 he was living in an old person's home, but continued to write and attempted to have his stories published. Also among his papers I found scripts he had written for television. The scripts appear to be segments for a children's program where 'Johnno' comes on (Compere: 'Well look boys and girls, it's Johnno the Deep Sea Diver') and recounts some of his adventures to a boy called Peter (possibly intended to be his grandson of the same name). Episode Five begins:

AFTERWORD

Peter: Johnno, have you ever seen a Mermaid?

Johnno: A mermaid. Good gracious me, Peter. Never. There is no such thing. Why, that is an old sailors yarn.

Peter: Well how about sea serpents? Have you seen them? The Loch Ness Monster for instance.

Johnno: No son. They're just old sailors' yarns too, every one of them.

Peter: Well then, what can you tell us about? You did promise a story about a ship that sank with a lot of gold.

Johnno: So I did. The ocean liner that struck a mine and sank with boxes and boxes of gold . . .

And from here the script has Johnno telling an obviously wide-eyed Peter the details of how the *Niagara*'s gold was recovered.

Throughout this book I have attempted, as much as is practical, to let the people involved in the story tell it in their own words, whether verbally or through their writing.

Now, with it necessary to bring the story to an end, I can think of no more appropriate way than to quote in full the last question and answer of the script that John Johnstone wrote shortly before his death:

Peter: What became of the gold? Was it yours to keep?

Johnno: Oh! No! We had to give it back to the Bank of England, which never ever rewarded us for our work! In fact the gold went over to America and was put deep down under the ground in the vaults of Fort Knox. We took it from the deep blue sea, only for it to be put in a deep hole in the ground. Aren't people funny? So long Peter, that's all.

Acknowledgments

I interviewed four men who served on the *Claymore*. They were Arthur Bryant, Jim Kemp, Les Mischewski and Ray Nelson. I thank each of them for giving their time and sharing their memories. I would also like to thank the families of Captain Sir John Williams, Captain James Herd, John E. Johnstone and Bill Johnstone, whose members trusted me on my word and willingly loaned me personal family papers, photographs and film. To compile this list of acknowledgments I've retraced my steps over five years of correspondence and notes, but if I have inadvertently missed someone I apologise to them.

I would like to thank the following people and organisations who assisted with this book.

Air New Zealand, J.H. Aitken, Peg Allen, Australian Archives, Margaret Bailey, Vince Ballenger, Bank of England, Nancy Bryant, Claudia Butcher, Dale Cave, Jim Chisholm, Alan Colquhuon, Commonwealth Bank of Australia, W. D. Comtesse, Thora Danaher, Peter Dennerly, Warwick Dunsford, Hugh Edwards, Jean Estall, Vaughan Evan, Joe Gough, Robert Greaves, C.D. Harrison, Angela Higgins, Vic Hill, Michael Hyland, David V. Isaacs, Phillip Isaacs, Bob Johnstone, Margo Johnstone, Peter Johnstone, Kelly Tarlton's Shipwreck Museum, Cecily Kemp, Frank Kowalewski, Kasper Kuiper-Tiffin, Roberta Kuiper-Tiffin, Lloyds of London, Ian Lockley, Roy Martin, Rebecca Maynard, Warren Maynard, Pat McCarthy, Ralph McDonell, John McLeod, J. D. McPherson, Gorden Miller, V.F. Morrisby, Paul Murphy, Joyce Nalder, National Archives of New Zealand, National Maritime Museum of New Zealand, Cecily Nelson, Tony Nesbit, J. Nills, Bill Reynolds, Reserve Bank of Australia, G. A. Robinson, Tony Rogers, Ken Ross, Mary Sanson, Glen Satchell, Kathy Satchell, Ken Scadden, Bill Scott, David Scott, John Siggins, Brian Sloper, Ken Smales, Roger Stephens, David Stevens, Alex Szecsenyi, Barbara Taggart, J. Thompson, John Thomson, Audrey Trimmer, Victorian Public Records Office, Lynette Vondruska, Peter West-Hill, J.E. Wilkinson, Jill Williams, Jim Williams, A.J. Wilson, Bruce Young.

References

BOOKS:

- Bromby, Robin, *German Raiders of the South Seas*, Doubleday Australia, 1985.
- Dunne, R.J. *Niagara Gold*, A.H & A.W. Reed, Wellington, 1942.
- Ingram, C.W.N., *New Zealand Shipwrecks*, A.H. & A.W. Reed, Wellington, 1977.
- Johnstone, J.E. and Peter Dawlish, *Johnno the Deep Sea Diver*, George Harrap & Co., London, 1960.
- Schmalenbach, Paul, *German Raiders*, Patrick Stephens, Cambridge, 1979.
- Scott, David, *Seventy Fathoms Deep*, Faber and Faber Ltd., London, 1931.
- Taylor, James, *Gold from the Sea*, Australasian Publishing Company, Sydney, 1942.
- Taylor, James, *Spoils from the Sea*, Australasian Publishing Company, Sydney, 1949.
- Waters, Sydney, *Union Line*, Union Line Publication.
- Weyher, Kurt, (and Hans Jurgen Ehrlich), *The Black Raider*, Elek Books, London, 1955.
- Williams, Captain Sir John, *So Ends This Day*, Globe Press, Melbourne, 1981.

OTHER SOURCES:

- The diary of Captain James Herd, Herd Family Collection
- Letters of Captain James Herd, Herd Family Collection
- Johnstone, J.E. 'Wrecks Was My Business', 1974, unpublished manuscript, Author's Collection.
- Johnstone, J.E. 'Diver's Yarns', unpublished manuscript, Johnstone Family Collection.
- The logbook of Salvage Vessel *Claymore*, Williams Family Collection
- Diary of Sister H. Munroe, Kelly Tarlton's Shipwreck Museum, Bay of Islands, New Zealand.
- General Correspondence, David V. Isaacs, Isaacs Family collection.

ARCHIVES:

National Archives of New Zealand:
- N1 6/36/1 – Loss of HMNZS *Puriri*
- N1 6/34 – Merchant Ships Lost
- N1 6/34/1 – Loss of RMS *Niagara*
- N1 6/20/2 – Claymore

Reserve Bank of Australia:
- S-a-1323 – Correspondence re *Niagara*, 1945-1952
- S-a-1313 – Gold, *Niagara*, Salvage – Remuneration to Syndicate
- S-a-1327 – Gold, *Niagara*, Salvage – Reports 1940, 41
- S-a-1311 – Gold, *Niagara*, Salvage – Agreement with United Salvage Syndicate
- S-a-1315 – Gold, *Niagara*, Salvage – Publicity of story and censorship
- S-a-1321 – Gold, *Niagara*, Salvage – Bank of England Reports
- S-a-1312 – Gold, *Niagara*, Salvage – Reports and statements of expenditure from Syndicate
- S-a-1314 – Gold, *Niagara*, Salvage – Interest of Whatmore, Thomson and Austin
- S-a-1316 – Gold, *Niagara*, Salvage – Reserve Bank of England and New Zealand, Payments
- S-a-1316 – Gold, *Niagara*, Salvage – Newspaper cuttings
- S-a-1318 – Gold, *Niagara*, Salvage – Custody of gold salved
- S-a-1333 – Gold, *Niagara*, Salvage – V. Neilley reports to bank.
- S-a-1327 – Gold, *Niagara*, Salvage – Williams reports to bank.

Australian Archives:
- Accession MP1587, File 164E – 'German Naval Operations in Australasia,'
- Accession MP278, Series 1, File c3/4 – Right to Salvage
- Accession A601, File 150/1/8 *Niagara* correspondence
- Accession MP 456/4, File 1944/228 – Observation Bell as used on *Niagara*.
- Series CRS A472, Item W1174 – *Niagara*, Loss of.
- Series A 571, Item 1940/3696 – Herd correspondence
- Series CRS A461, Item AG418/2/9 – Recovery of Gold from *Niagara*
- Series A571, Item 1940/3696 – *Niagara* censorship/Taxation of bonuses.
- Series A5954, Item 329/16 – Censorship concerning *Niagara* salvage operations.

Victorian Public Records Office:
- Series No. 7972P1 Box 290 – S.S. *Kakariki*.

Australian Securities Commission:
- C22399S – Incorporation of United Salvage.

Index

Achilles, HMNZS 21
Adelaide, South Australia 134
Africa 121
Alcock, Joe 35, 90
Allen, Peg 81
Antarctica 140
Anti-Comintern Pact 9, 108
anti-paralysis diving suit 71, 73, 94
Arrol, Sir Wm. 34
Asia 107
Atlantic Ocean 14, 17
Atlantis (Raider) 11
Auckland 18, 19, 22, 36, 41, 42, 51, 52, 54, 58, 59, 86, 88, 91, 92, 95, 97, 99, 117, 124, 146
Auckland Harbour 12, 13, 16, 18, 36, 38, 39, 123, 143
Auckland Harbour Board 26
Auckland Police 21
Aurora 140.
AUSN Company 88
Austin, W.F. 93, 94
Austral Submarine Inventions Ltd 72
Australasian Post 7, 8, 40
Australia 10, 11, 14, 17, 27, 30, 32, 38, 41, 57, 72-74, 88, 91, 93, 113, 115, 117, 132, 133, 135, 144, 146
Australia, HMAS 95
Australian High Commissioner 139
Australian Labor Party 117
Australian Military forces 142
Australian National (Shipping) Line 152
Australian National Maritime Museum 149
Australian Naval Board 22, 24, 73
Australian Navy 17, 27, 28, 35, 73, 95, 112
Australian Navy Reserve 24, 25
Autralasian Antarctic Expedition 140

Bank of England 16, 22, 27, 37, 93, 126, 128, 139, 141, 142, 145, 146, 148, 153.
Bank of New Zealand 122, 123, 124
Barwick, Sir Garfield 149
Battle of Britain 21, 56
Bay of Islands (New Zealand) 19, 84, 104, 149
Belfast 60
Betsy (tender) 62, 66, 75
Bingley, Commander 41, 52, 53, 58, 117, 118
Branch, Fred 80

Bream Head 75, 97
British Admiralty 22, 73, 89
British Army 10
British Commonwealth 10
British Government 74
British Islands 10, 56
Briton, Commander J.E. 97
Brown & Co., John 15
Bryant, Arthur J. 8, 34, 35, 40, 46, 48-50, 53, 58, 83, 90-92, 123, 134
Bulletin, The 135
Burns and Co 37

Campbell, Mrs 95
Canada 10, 14, 15, 18
Cape Horn 13
Cape of Good Hope 17
Caradale s.s. 25
Caroline Islands 17
Casey Antarctic Base 141
Castlemaine, Victoria 29, 31, 149
Chadwick, Harold 146
Chaucer (MV) 17
Chicken Islands Light 51
Chifley, Ben 144
Childs, Diver 95
China 107, 108
Christchurch NZ 14
Churchill, Winston 10, 21
Claymore, Salvage Vessel 40-66, 68, 69, 71, 73, 74, 75, 77-82, 84, 86, 88-92, 94-99, 102, 103, 106, 108-116, 118, 122-132, 138, 140, 142-146, 152.
– fitting out 36, 37, 38
– logbook 39, 46, 49-51, 53, 53, 54, 63, 65, 67, 75, 84, 85, 105, 106, 110, 115, 116, 122, 124, 129, 131
– crew, bonuses paid to 100, 101
Clifford, Ernest 71-73
Colville Channel 76
Commonwealth Bank of Australia 22, 27, 28, 29, 41, 59, 75, 93, 94, 100, 106, 113, 117, 122-124, 126-128, 139, 141, 142, 146
Commonwealth Government 142
Commonwealth Salvage Board 143
Coombes, Dr 139
Cormoran (Raider) 11
Cornwall, HMS 11
Crown Solicitor 142
Cumberland s.s. 146
Curtin, John 117, 139, 140, 142, 144
Cuvier lighthouse 14
Czechoslovakia 9

Danaher, Thora 92
da Vinci, Leonardo 71
Darwin 133, 134, 135, 143
Davis, John K. 136-138, 140, 141
Davis, Sidney Hyam 37, 38, 93, 94, 95, 127
Davis, Sir Ernest 37, 95
Deloraine, HMAS 133
Department of Commerce (Aust.) 135, 136, 138
Devonport Naval Base 123
Dianton, Stan 80, 90
Diole, Philippe 143
Discovery 140
Distinguished Service Cross 138
Dover Breakwater 34
Duchess, HMNZS Minesweeper 42
Dunkirk, 10

Edward I (King of England) 89
Egypt s.s. 31, 92, 112, 138
Egypt 121
Egypt's Gold (book) 31, 88
Emden (Raider) 11
Emirau 17, 18
England 140, 145, 148
English Channel 10, 56
Europe 57, 107, 108
Eyssen, Robert 17

Fadden, Arthur 117
Fairfax Group 7, 135
Fairfax, Warwick 114
Fiji 15
Flinders Naval Base 28
Forde, R.M. 135
Foremost 17 146-148
Fort Knox 153
France 9, 10, 17
Friedrich (Raider) 11

Gale, HMNZS Auxiliary Minesweeper 76, 97
George II (King of England) 89
George III (King of England) 89
German Army 10
German Navy 12.
Germany 9, 10, 11, 16, 23, 107, 108
Gibson, Chief Officer 52
Glasgow, Scotland 15
Glenfine South Mine 144
Goble, Air Vice-Marshall S.J. 15
Goble, Mrs 15
Goodwin Sands, 34
Great Barrier Island 76
Great Britain 9, 10, 11, 24, 57, 107, 108, 117, 132
Green, Bill 34, 35, 62, 90, 91

Hamburg-America Line 12
Hartnett, L.J. 135, 136
Hauraki Gulf 13, 14, 15, 18, 68, 76, 77, 95, 96, 98, 104
Hawaii 131
Haxby (MV) 13
Haynes, Lieutenant 112
Hebdon, Zoe 40
Hen and Chickens Islands 19, 74, 83, 98, 110
Herd, Captain James 55, 56, 58, 60, 62, 69, 79-82, 84, 90-92, 103, 107, 112, 113, 120, 124, 129, 130, 132, 139, 140
Higgins, Frank 146
Hillington, Captain 113
Hitler, Adolf, 9, 10, 16, 21, 57
Holden, Commander 54, 61
Holland 10
Holmwood s.s. 17
Hull, England 23
Humphrey, HMNZS Minesweeper 45, 46, 48, 49, 50, 51, 52

Idriess, Ion 114
India 10
Indian Ocean 17
Inkster, Dr J.G. 15
Inkster, Mrs 15
Inverness, (Barque) 23
Isaacs, David V. 31-34, 65, 99, 131, 149
Italy 108

Japan 9, 72, 107, 108, 132
Japanese submarines (I-124, I-123) 133, 134
Jervis Bay 135
Johnstone, Bill 8, 34, 35, 41, 45, 69, 79, 90, 102, 107, 108, 109, 112, 119, 130, 131, 134, 151
Johnstone, John E. 9, 25, 26, 34-51, 54, 55, 56, 58, 63-67, 69, 72, 75, 76, 79, 80, 81, 82, 84, 86, 90, 96, 99, 101-105, 107, 112, 114, 116, 118-120, 124, 125, 128-130, 134, 139, 141, 142, 144-148, 151-153
Johnstone, Peter 152, 153

Kakariki s.s. 25, 26
kauri tree 84, 85
Kelly Tarlton's Shipwreck Museum, 104, 149
Kemp, Jim 88, 90, 91, 92, 96, 101, 109, 110, 116, 126, 141, 143, 148
King John (MV) 23
Kiorera Wharf 61
Komet (Raider) 17, 18
Korea 107
Kurmark 12

INDEX

Laurentic 138
Le Noury, John 72
League of Nations 108
Leonard, J.M. 115, 117, 118, 134
Lithuania 9
London 17, 57, 139, 148
Long, R.B.M. (Cocky) 95
Lowe, Nipper 80, 90
Luftwaffe 56
Luxembourg 10

Manaia Gardens Guest House 54, 81, 123
Maori s.s. 14
Maori people 84, 85
Market Museum, Castlemaine 29, 149
Maro Tiri Islands 53
Marshall Islands 17
Martin, Captain William 16, 19, 20
Maryborough, Victoria 8
Mawson Antarctic Base 141
Mawson, Sir Douglas 140
Maynard, Jeff 8
McDonald Hamilton 88
McKay, Donald 88, 113, 114, 126, 127
McLeod, Commander Cathel 97, 98
Meiji Restoration 107
Melbourne Harbour Trust 26
Melbourne, Australia 7, 8, 14, 22, 28, 41, 60, 71, 72, 73, 95, 100, 101, 118, 133, 134, 141, 144
Memel 9
Menai, s.s. 52
Menzies, Robert 35, 57, 117
Merchant Shipping Act 90
Military Intelligence, Australian 72, 94
Mills, James 14
mine, German Y-type 18, 43-51, 53, 54, 104
Minister of War Expenditure (NZ) 144
Miowera RMS 15
Mischewski, Les 60, 61, 90, 151, 152
Mitchell, Stan 34, 61, 80, 90
Moko Hinau Light 51
Moravia 9
Muir and Houston 68
Munroe, Sister H. 20
Muritai, HMNZS Minesweeper 54, 61
Mussolini, Benito 138

Nalder, Tommy 91, 92, 131, 132
Nauru 17
Naval Board of Enquiry (NZ) 97, 98
Naval Intelligence, Australian 75, 127
Neilley, Victor 106, 111, 118, 124-126, 131
Neilson, Lieutenant 45, 49, 50

Nelson, Ray 19, 37, 44, 53, 55, 63, 91, 120, 123, 142
New Caledonia 17, 73, 74.
New Guinea 145
New York 60
New York Explorers Club 152
New Zealand 8, 10,11, 12, 13, 14, 26, 34, 35, 38, 40, 41, 42, 55, 73, 74, 77, 84, 85, 88, 93, 95, 99, 106, 114, 115, 122, 131, 144, 145, 149
New Zealand Government 59
New Zealand Minister of Defence 59
New Zealand Naval Board 52, 59, 111
New Zealand Navy 51, 58, 60, 61, 76, 97, 98, 99, 104, 111, 112, 117, 122, 127, 143
Niagara Falls 15
Niagara, RMS 14-16, 24-27, 30, 35, 36, 38, 42, 51, 52, 54, 56-60, 62, 64, 66, 68, 70, 71, 73-79, 82, 83, 86, 88-90, 93-96, 98, 102-104, 108, 109, 112, 115, 122, 125, 128, 132, 134, 135, 137, 139, 140, 143-149, 152, 153
– sinking 18-22
Nimrod 140
Nobels of London 84
North Atlantic 11, 13
Notou (MV) 17

Observation Chamber (bell) 38, 42-44, 63-67, 69-71, 75, 78, 79, 82, 85, 86, 99, 100, 102-106, 108, 109, 112, 116-119, 131, 149
– design and construction 29-34
Order of the British Empire 138
Orion (Raider) 12, 13, 15, 16, 17, 18, 76, 98

Pacific Ocean 14, 15, 22, 57, 107, 108, 117, 131, 143
Paracelsus 137
Paris 10
Paulson, Max 35, 46, 54, 57, 88
Pearl Harbour 131, 134
Pearline 97
Perry, Commander Mathew 107
Philippines 133
Phoney War, The 9, 10
Pinguin 11
Plaza Theatre, 92, 152
Poland 9
Port of Melbourne 25
Port Phillip Heads 72
Port Said 23
Prime Minister's Department (Aust) 137, 138
Prinz Eitel (Raider) 11
Puriri, HMNZS Auxiliary Minesweeper 76, 97, 98

Rand 16
Rangitane RMS 17
Rawea HMNZS 97
Regent Theatre, Whangarei 61
Reynolds, Bill 21, 51
Rigby, Bluey 90, 132
Ringwood 17
Risdon-Beazley salvage group 146
Ross Sea 140
Royal Air Force 56
Royal Mail 14
Royal New Zealand Air Force 13
Russia 107

Salvage Law 89, 90
Sanson, Mary 40-41
Schimdt, Seaman Paul 13
Schleswig-Holstein 13
Scotland 15, 38, 68
Scott, Danny 7, 8, 35, 40, 44, 46, 60, 63, 79, 132, 151
Scott, David 31, 88
Seagers Shipbuilding Yard 36
Seaman's Union 88
Secretary of the Treasury 142
Security Service, Australian 95, 127
Seeadler (Raider) 11
Shackleton Ice Shelf 141
Shackleton, Sir Ernest 137, 140
Shain, G.M. 28, 41, 100, 118
Sheehan, Sir Harry, 28
Sicamous RMS 15
Singapore 131
South Africa 10, 16
South Pacific 11, 12,13
South Pole 140
South Sea, HMNZS Minesweeper 42
Southern Hemisphere 10, 111, 146
Sudetan 9.
Sydney, Australia 14, 16, 17,18, 19, 37, 38, 55, 72, 75, 133
Sydney Harbour 73
Sydney Morning Herald 7, 114, 134, 135

Tasman Sea 14
Taylor, James 114, 115, 117-120, 134
Theodore, Ted 37
Thompson, John 35, 46, 54, 57, 73, 88
Thompsons Engineering and Pipe Co. 31
Thomson, William 73-75, 93, 94, 127
Times Atlas of World War Two 143
Titanic s.s. 15
Tobruk 135
Tokyo 107

Torres Strait 133
Trans-Pacific Telephone Cable 96
Tripartite Pact 108
Tropic Sea (MV), 16, 17
Turakina (MV) 17

U-boat 11, 23
Union Steamship Company 14, 15, 25, 82
United Salvage 25, 26, 27, 28, 29, 39, 88, 106, 113, 114, 141, 142, 144
United States Navy 107
United States of America 10, 15, 16, 21, 60, 107, 108, 117, 128, 132
United Stevedoring Pty Ltd 26, 136
Urquharts Bay, NZ 45, 53, 54, 61, 78, 79, 81, 97, 123
Uther, A.W. 73-75

Wanganella, RMS 22
War Council (NZ) 41
Warren, Alf 34, 46, 79, 90, 134
Warrington School of Dancing 92
Warrington, Claudia 92
Washington Naval Treaty 107
Wellington 13, 14, 52, 53, 58
Wellington Maritime Museum 149
Western Australia 8, 72
Western Europe 10
Western Independent 7
Weyher, Kurt 12,13, 16, 17, 18
Whangarei 21, 39, 40, 41, 42, 45, 51, 52, 54, 57-61, 75, 76, 79, 81, 83, 85, 86, 88, 91, 92, 99, 106, 111, 116, 117, 122-128, 132, 151
Whangarei Harbour 61, 81
Whangarei Harbour Board 40, 127
Whangarei Heads 21, 42, 80
Whangarei Police 21
Whatmore, Henry 72,-75, 93, 94, 127
Whatmore-Thomson-Uther salvage syndicate 93
Wilkinson, Lieutenant-Commander 94, 95
Williams, Gladys 95, 127
Williams, Captain J.P. 8, 9, 31, 35-66, 68-71, 73-86, 88, 90, 91, 94, 95, 98-104, 106-115, 117-120, 122, 123, 124, 126-132, 134-139, 141, 143,-146, 149, 151, 152.
– formation of salvage syndicate 25-29
– career 23-25.
– formation of crew 34, 35
Wise MLC, Wilfred & Mrs Wise 15
Wolf (Raider) 11
World War One 11, 12, 23, 76, 107, 138
World War Two 10, 11, 12, 24

Young, Dick 146